THE OLDER AMERICANS COOKBOOK

by

Marilyn McFarlane

Preface by Carolyn Ostergren, R.D.

Tudor Publishers, Inc.   Greensboro

THE OLDER AMERICANS COOKBOOK

Printed in the United States of America

First printing, September 1988

LIBRARY OF CONGRESS CATALOGING-IN-PUBLICATION DATA

McFarlane, Marilyn.
    The Older Americans cookbook / by Marilyn McFarlane; preface by Carolyn Ostergren.
    p.   cm.
ISBN 0-936389-04-4: $16.95.   ISBN 0-936389-05-2 (pbk.): $8.95   ISBN 0-936389-06-0 (comb bd.):
    1. Cookery.   2. Aged—Nutrition.   I. Title.
TX652.M366 1988
641.5′627—dc19   88-16923
                                                                                      CIP

Author's note: Every reasonable effort has been made to ascertain that the recipes in this book are original and unique. Should there be any question concerning this, please notify the publisher so that proper credit can be given in any subsequent editions.

PUBLISHER'S NOTE: The recipes and meal plans contained herein should in no way substitute for the advice and counsel of a physician. Any person with special dietary or health needs should consult a physician before changing their dietary regimen.

88 89 90   54321

To the memory of my mother
Ida Mary McFarlane

Acknowledgements

Without the help of numerous people who are interested in the nutritional needs of senior citizens, this book could not have been written.

My heartfelt thanks go to those who contributed suggestions from their own files and memories, especially those residents of Rose Villa Retirement Home who shared their stories and recipes.

I am deeply grateful to Carolyn Ostergren for her generosity and expertise. She not only offered professional opinions on the book's content, but also provided suggestions on recipes, menus and tips that greatly enhance the usefulness of The Older Americans Cookbook. As a dietitian with extensive experience in the field of nutrition and aging, her advice was invaluable.

Thanks for their assistance and suggestions are owed to Kay Girsberger, R.D., Food Service manager at Rose Villa, Inc., and Nancy Thorn, R.D., dietitian for Kaiser Permanente Clinic.

I also wish to thank Myrna Oakley, Gail Denham, and Sharon Wood, who provided support, enthusiasm and ideas.

A special thank you to my aunt, Esther MacLaren, for her help in contributing and collecting recipes.

Finally, thanks to my husband, John Parkhurst, for his unflagging good humor and willingness to participate in many weeks of recipe testing.

Preface

Maintaining a "quality life" in our later years—a life brimming with health, energy, mental alertness and productivity—is of great value. And to a degree that surprises some people, such a life is possible. Many people find that their older years are just as satisfying and vigorous as their younger days, and sometimes more so.

To maintain such a quality life, a good diet is essential. A sound, nutritious, balanced diet can minimize health problems and provide the sense of well-being that makes life seem worth living. However, with the changing circumstances that come with age, dietary needs shift. Health and digestive problems may arise, and sodium and cholesterol intake may have to be lowered. Finances may be limited and food budgets tightened. Lifestyles change as families shrink in size. Preparing meals for one or two requires a big adjustment after cooking for a larger family.

The Older Americans Cookbook addresses these issues in a straightforward and readable manner. Each recipe and menu has been checked against the latest dietary knowledge and tested for both nutritional value and for flavor. Many older people who have been successful at keeping their diets healthy and interesting have contributed their ideas, learned from long experience, to the book. Their suggestions have been used extensively throughout the book, which is designed to be not only a collection of recipes, but a general nutritional guide that will help make "quality living" a reachable goal.

— *Carolyn Ostergren*
Registered Dietitian
Oregon Health Sciences University

Table of Contents

Introduction/How To Use This Book

It was just noon on a blustery Saturday in March when I stopped by my widowed mother's apartment to say hello. She was eating lunch—half a slice of white bread, a small piece of cheese, and a cup of tea.

"That's not much lunch," I said as I removed my coat.

"I know," she answered with a guilty smile. Then she sighed. "But I can't think of anything else to fix and don't have the energy anyway. Neither do most of my friends."

It was then, as I put on an apron and began preparing a hot, tasty vegetable soup, that I decided to write this book.

Eating good food is one of life's greatest pleasures. That enjoyment shouldn't stop at a certain age; it should continue on into our golden years. Our bodies may require less food to maintain life and energy, but we still need nutrients, fiber and flavorsome meals. The food we eat, and the way we eat it, contribute greatly to the quality of our lives. Eating well is *important!*

Many older people lose interest in food. They may have trouble chewing or have physical problems that make it difficult to meet their dietary needs. They may be low on energy, or they may be bored. With no one but herself to cook for, the woman living alone often neglects her own meals. The man alone may not know how to prepare a proper meal.

The Older Americans Cookbook was created to change all that. It's packed with recipes, menu ideas and helpful hints. In an easy-to-read, easy-to-use format, it provides six weeks' worth of flavorful menus and simple, fast cooking methods.

We haven't neglected nutrition in preparing this cookbook. All the menus and recipes have been carefully reviewed by a dietitian who specializes in geriatric nutrition. Many of the recipes were developed by senior citizens who are looking for shortcuts in meal preparation but do not wish to sacrifice taste and enjoyment.

The pages of this book also contain useful extras, such as hints for shopping and cooking and fitness. You'll find suggestions for those on tight budgets, for people on low-sodium or low-cholesterol diets, and for people who live alone and usually eat alone. All these problems are surmountable. They require some creativity and effort, but the results are worth it. Nothing means more to a high quality of life than the food we consume.

How To Use This Book

The Older Americans Cookbook is divided into, first, a Recipe Section, and second, a Suggested Menus Section.

Almost every dish in the "Recipes" section is included in one or more of the menus in the "Suggested Menus" section. You may choose to try a recipe that seems appealing, or you may wish to follow the recommended menu that uses that dish.

In the "Menus" section, you will find both *light* and *hearty* menus for breakfasts and dinners for a six week period. The foods were selected for their combinations of flavor, texture and nutrition, though you may prefer to substitute your own favorites in some cases.

Most of the recipes are in quantities that serve one or two people. However, they are easy to increase or decrease, according to the number of servings you need, by doubling or halving the ingredients. All ingredients are generally available throughout the United States and easy to obtain, depending upon the region and season.

You may notice that most of the recipes call for very little, if any, salt or sugar but plenty of herbs, spices and fiber. These healthy, taste-enhancing foods combine deliciously, so there is no loss of flavor—in fact, you will find that they improve the flavor and variety of your diet.

Because seasonings are so important to these recipes, we are providing suggestions for easy ways to use them. Many recipes call for one of our special seasoning combinations: either Mixed Herbs, Mixed Hot Spices, or Mixed Sweet Spices. Fix up a batch of each, store them in tightly-closed containers, and you'll be ready for a quick and tasty recipe.

Mixed Herbs

(Makes about 1/3 cup)

3 tablespoons dried sweet basil
1 tablespoon dried marjoram
1 teaspoon dried thyme
1 teaspoon dried oregano

★   ★   ★

Mixed Hot Spices

3 tablespoons chili powder
1-1/2 teaspoons cumin
3/4 teaspoon cayenne pepper
1/4 teaspoon turmeric

★   ★   ★

Mixed Sweet Spices

3 tablespoons cinnamon
1-1/2 teaspoons allspice
1-1/2 teaspoons ground cloves
3/4 teaspoon ground ginger
3/4 teaspoon ground nutmeg
3/4 teaspoon mace

Section One

RECIPES

B_{EE}F

§ One-Pot Pot Roast §
(Serves 2, with leftovers)

Hearty beef and vegetable goodness prepared in a single pot. You can add more vegetables, too—fresh or frozen peas, green beans, or other favorites. Save the leftovers for tomorrow's meal.

> 2 pound boneless beef chuck roast
> 2 teaspoons beef bouillon granules or 2 bouillon cubes, mixed with 1/2 cup water
> 2 tablespoons lemon juice
> 1/2 cup wine, red or white (optional)
> 1 small onion, sliced
> 1 carrot, sliced
> 1 potato, sliced (peel if you prefer)
> 1 clove garlic, pressed or minced
> 1 teaspoon Mixed Herbs
> Bay leaf
> 1/4 teaspoon pepper

Preheat oven to 350°.
Place beef in baking dish.
Pour bouillon, lemon juice and wine over meat.
Sprinkle with herbs and pepper.
Add vegetables and cover
Bake 1-1/2 hours, until tender.

Tempt Your Appetite
When food and eating seem a bore, there are several ways to perk up your appetite. Suggestions:
—Take a walk. Even a short walk outside will stimulate your circulation and appetite.
—Set a special table. A pretty placement, a candle, a cloth napkin and "company" china can make a meal seem more appealing, whether you dine alone or with others.

§ Meat and Potatoes §
(Serves 1)

For those who love a stick-to-the-ribs standby.

1/2 cup cooked, diced beef roast
1/2 cup beef gravy (packaged or left over)
1/4 cup cooked, mashed potatoes (instant packaged
   potatoes allow trouble-free preparation, but are higher in
   sodium)
2 tablespoons milk
1 teaspoon butter or margarine
1/2 cup cooked carrots or peas
1/2 teaspoon Mixed Herbs

Preheat oven to 350°.
Mix beef with gravy in baking dish.
Add all other ingredients.
Stir and bake 15 minutes.

§ "Yoganoff" with Zucchini §
(Serves 2)

Enid Byron shares this taste-pleaser with her neighbors and gets
rave reviews. The stroganoff-like sauce is based on lower-calorie
yogurt. (For authentic stroganoff, Enid uses sour cream instead of
yogurt.)

1/2 pound sirloin or filet of beef, cut in strips
1 tablespoon vegetable oil
1 clove garlic, minced
1/2 cup fresh mushrooms, sliced
1 tablespoon butter or margarine
1 tablespoon flour
3/4 cup beef bouillon

2 tablespoons white wine (optional)
1 teaspoon catsup
1/2 cup sliced zucchini
1/4 teaspoon dill
1/4 cup plain yogurt

Sauté beef in oil in skillet, browning all sides.
Add garlic and mushrooms and sauté lightly.
Remove beef, garlic and mushrooms from pan and set aside.
Melt butter and add flour and catsup, stirring until smooth.
Add bouillon and simmer, stirring until thickened.
Add wine, beef and mushrooms, cover and simmer 45-60 minutes, until tender.
Add zucchini and cook another 5 minutes.
Stir in dill and yogurt and heat. Do not boil.

§ "No-Peek" Stew §
(Serves 2)

From a superb cook who enjoys an occasional no-trouble meal comes this unusual dish. Edith Owenbey puts it in the oven at lunchtime and its ready by evening. "The result is like something from a crockpot," she says.

1/2 pound lean stew beef, cut in bite-sized pieces
1 potato
1 carrot
Other vegetables, as desired.
1 can tomato soup, undiluted

Mix all ingredients and place in baking dish.
Cover and place in cold oven.
Turn oven to 250° and leave for 5 hours. If more liquid is desired add water.

§ Raisin Beef §
(Serves 2)

1 tablespoon vegetable oil
3/4 pound lean beef, cut in cubes
2 cloves garlic, minced
1 teaspoon Mixed Herbs
4 tablespoons liquid from canned tomatoes, or water
1 potato, peeled and sliced
1 carrot, sliced
Pinch nutmeg
1/4 cup raisins
1/2 cup canned tomatoes, drained (or fresh, chopped)

Sauté beef cubes in skillet until browned on all sides.
Add garlic, Mixed Herbs and liquid.
Cover tightly and simmer 30 minutes. Add more liquid if desired.
Add potato and carrot slices, cover and simmer 20 minutes, until
  meat and vegetables are tender.
Stir in tomatoes, raisins and nutmeg. Simmer, uncovered, until sauce
  thickens.

§ Snappy Ginger Beef §
(Serves 2)

2 slices bacon
1/2 onion, chopped
1/2 cup beef broth or bouillon
1/4 cup crushed ginger snap cookies
2 tablespoons brown sugar
1 tablespoon vinegar
3/4 cup cooked beef, cut in cubes

Sauté bacon in skillet until crisp. Remove bacon and crumble.
Place all other ingredients except beef in skillet.
Add bacon and simmer 10 minutes.
Add beef cubes and simmer until heated through.

§ Moon's Minestrone Soup §
(Serves 6-8)

A university professor, "Moon" often shares this favorite recipe with his students. He advises cooking "lots of soup; it's good the next day and easy to freeze for later."

4 cups water
1-1/2 pounds beef with bone (or stew meat)
1/4 cup kidney beans
1/2 teaspoon salt
2 bay leaves
1/4 cup chopped celery
1 onion, sliced
1/2 teaspoon hot pepper sauce
1 16-ounce can tomatoes
1 cup shredded cabbage
3 carrots, sliced
1/2 cup vermicelli pasta
1 cup frozen peas
1 zucchini, sliced
Parmesan cheese, grated

Combine water, beef, beans, salt and bay leaves in kettle.
Heat to boiling and skim foam.
Cover and simmer 2 hours.
Add celery, onion, hot sauce, cabbage, tomatoes and carrots and
    simmer 30 minutes.
Add vermicelli, peas, and zucchini and simmer 15 minutes.
Remove bay leaves and serve, topped with Parmesan cheese.

§ Swiss Steak Special §
(Serves 2 generously)

Vegetables and meat cook together in a tomato-garlic sauce, combining flavors to create a superb meal in a single pot.

1/2 pound round steak or flank steak
1 tablespoon flour
1/4 teaspoon pepper
1/2 onion, sliced
2 garlic cloves, pressed or minced
2 tablespoons vegetable oil
1 bay leaf
1/2 teaspoon Mixed Herbs
1 potato, chopped
1 carrot, chopped
2/3 cup tomato juice (or combined tomato sauce and water)
1/2 teaspoon vinegar

Rub flour and pepper on steak.
Lightly brown onion and garlic in 1 tablespoon hot oil in skillet.
Remove from pan and set aside.
Brown steak on both sides in 1 tablespoon oil in skillet.
Add onion, seasonings, tomato juice and vinegar.
Cover and simmer 1 hour, adding more liquid if needed.
Arrange potatoes and carrots around meat.
Cover and simmer 30 minutes.

Buy Double, Save Trouble
When a recipe calls for one-half pound of ground beef, buy a full pound and make hamburger patties with the other half. Separate the patties with waxed paper and freeze for another meal.

§ Oriental Beef §
(Serves 2)

Crisp vegetables, tender beef, and the tang of ginger combine to create the flavor of the Orient. Substitute other vegetables according to taste: green beans, broccoli, water chestnuts and asparagus are good choices.

    1 tablespoon vegetable oil
    10-12 strips lean beef
    2 tablespoons sliced onions
    1 carrot, cut diagonally
    1 celery stalk, cut diagonally
    1/4 cup green pepper chunks
    1 teaspoon chopped fresh ginger
    1 garlic clove, chopped or pressed
    1 cup beef broth or bouillon
    1 tablespoon cornstarch
    1 tablespoon soy sauce

Heat oil in skillet or wok.
Sauté beef strips until brown. Remove beef from pan.
Add vegetables and saute until tender but still crisp.
Stir in ginger and garlic.
Add broth or bouillon and beef, cover and simmer 5 minutes.
Mix cornstarch with soy sauce and add to beef mixture,
    stirring until thickened.

§ Meat Loaf §
(Serves 2, with leftovers)

A rich, beefy loaf with bread crumbs—easy to make by grating frozen French bread.

    1 egg
    1/2 pound lean ground beef

1/4 cup tomato sauce or stewed tomatoes
3 tablespoons bread crumbs
1 teaspoon soy sauce (optional)
2 tablespoons grated carrot
1 teaspoon lemon rind, grated or minced
1 clove garlic, pressed or minced
Dash pepper

Preheat oven to 375°.
Beat egg.
Add all other ingredients and mix with hands.
Place mixture in loaf pan.
Bake 45 minutes.

§ Beef 'N Beans §
(Serves 2)

1/2 pound lean ground beef
1 cup (9-ounce can) baked beans
1/2 cup crushed pineapple with juice
2 tablespoons brown sugar
1/4 cup catsup

Preheat oven to 350°.
Sauté ground beef in skillet until browned. Drain fat.
Add all other ingredients.
Pour into baking dish.
Bake 40 minutes.

Conserve Energy

On days when you have more energy, cook enough for more than one meal. Save the extras for the next day, or freeze to keep them for a day when you don't feel like cooking—or even thinking about it.

§ E-Z Ground Beef Casserole §
(Serves 2)

Esther MacLaren's one-dish meal is delicious and quick to fix-a good
hot dinner after an afternoon with her book club.

    1/2 pound lean ground beef
    1/2 onion, chopped
    1/4 cup white rice
    1-1/2 cups water or beef bouillon
    1 potato, peeled and cubed
    1 carrot, sliced
    1/4 teaspon salt
    Dash pepper
    2 teaspoons soy sauce

Preheat oven to 350°.
Brown beef and onion in skillet. Drain fat.
Mix all other ingredients, pour into baking dish.
Bake 30 minutes. (Dish may also be cooked on top of stove.)

§ Chili Hash §
(Serves 2)

Not too hot, not too mild— a beef chili dish that has a just-right
touch of spice.

    1/2 onion, chopped
    1/2 green bell pepper, chopped
    1/2 pound ground beef
    1 tablespoon vegetable oil
    1 cup tomato sauce
    1/2 cup water
    1/4 cup uncooked brown or white rice
    1/2 teaspoon chili powder

1/4 teaspoon oregano
Dash cumin
Dash pepper

Preheat oven to 350°.
Heat oil in skillet and sauté onion, green pepper and beef until
  lightly browned. Drain fat.
Stir in all other ingredients.
Pour into oiled baking dish.
Cover and bake one hour, until rice is tender.

§ Goulash §
(Serves 2 generously)

Vera Porter contributes this recipe for a hearty, flavorful one-dish
meal.

1/2 pound lean ground beef
1/2 cup cooked macaroni
2 tablespoons chopped green bell pepper
1 tablespoon steak sauce
1 cup (1 small can) cream-style corn
1/2 can tomato soup
Dash salt and pepper
1/2 cup grated cheddar cheese

Preheat oven to 350°.
Brown ground beef in skillet. Drain fat.
Add all other ingredients except cheese and stir.
Place in baking dish and sprinkle with cheese.
Bake 45 minutes.

§ Deep-Dish Spaghetti Bake §
(Serves 2, with leftovers)

4 ounces spaghetti, cooked
1/2 pound lean ground beef
1/2 onion, chopped
1/2 teaspoon salt
1 clove garlic, pressed or minced
1/4 teaspoon oregano
1 teaspoon sweet basil
Dash hot pepper sauce
1 16-ounce can stewed tomatoes
1/3 cup chopped mushrooms, canned or fresh
1/2 cup grated Parmesan or Romano cheese (or other favorite cheese)

Preheat oven to 375°.
Sauté ground beef in skillet until browned.
Add onion and sauté until tender. Drain fat.
Stir in remaining ingredients except spaghetti and cheese and bring to a simmer.
Stir in spaghetti.
Pour mixture into greased casserole and place in oven.
Bake 20 minutes.
Sprinkle with grated cheese and bake 5 more minutes.

Exercise

Healthful eating is an important part of maintaining physical fitness. Another part is regular exercise. Scientists say that you may reduce the risk of coronary heart disease by exercising enough to burn 2000 calories per week. You'll feel better, too. Walking, bicycling and swimming are ideal and pleasant forms of exercise. If you walk briskly for 30 minutes, you will expend 150 calories. A leisurely swim will burn 200 calories in 30 minutes, and half and hour of golf takes 125 calories. If you are not accustomed to exercise, start slowly. Ask you doctor which exercise or sports are best for you; then get out and enjoy yourself!

§ Spaghetti With Meat Sauce §
(Serves 2)

1/2 pound lean ground beef
1 tablespoon vegetable oil
1/2 onion, chopped
1/2 green pepper, chopped
1   8 ounce can stewed tomatoes or 1 can tomato paste
    with 3 cans water
2 cloves garlic, minced
1 teaspoon Mixed Herbs
1/2 teaspoon sugar (optional)
4 ounces spaghetti

Sauté ground beef and onions in oil in skillet until meat is browned.
  Drain fat.
Add all other ingredients except spaghetti.
Cover and simmer 2 hours, stirring occasionally. Add water if more
  liquid is needed.
Cook spaghetti in boiling water in kettle just until tender. Drain.
Serve sauce over spaghetti and sprinkle with Parmesan cheese, if
desired.

§ Stuffed Green Peppers §
(Serves 2)

2 green bell peppers
2 tablespoons chopped onion
1 tablespoon vegetable oil
1/2 pound lean ground beef
1/2 cup dry bread crumbs
2 tablespoons grated cheddar cheese
1 teaspoon Mixed Hot Spices

1/2 cup tomato sauce
2 tablespoons water

Preheat oven to 375°.
Slice top off peppers. Discard stem and chop trimmings. Remove
  seeds and membranes from peppers.
Blanch peppers (about 4 minutes in boiling water).
Heat oil in skillet. Sauté onion and pepper trimmings.
Add beef and sauté until browned. Remove from heat. Drain fat.
Mix crumbs, cheese and seasonings and add to beef mixture.
Spoon into peppers.
Place peppers in buttered baking dish.
Mix tomato sauce and water and pour over and around peppers.
Bake 30 minutes.

Stretching

Our bodies were made to move. When we don't stretch and move, we become less flexible and more prone to injury. Slow, easy stretching of our major muscle groups relieves tension and promotes agility.

You can stretch almost any time, anywhere. While watching television, for example, take regular breaks in which you consciously reach and stretch your arms and legs. Gently rotate your head; slowly raise and lower your shoulders; breathe deeply. You will feel a lovely sense of relaxation and well-being.

§ Hamburger Stew §
(Serves 2)

1/2 pound lean ground beef.
1 tablespoon vegetable oil
1/2 onion, chopped
1 celery stalk with leaves, chopped
1 patato, cubed, (peel if your prefer; it's not necessary)
1 garlic clove, sliced
1/4 teaspoon salt
Dash pepper
1 bay leaf
1 beef bouillon cube
2 cups water

Heat oil in saucepan.
Sauté ground beef in oil until browned. Drain fat.
Add all other ingredients.
Bring to a boil, then simmer for one-half hour, adding water
  if needed.

§ Prime Time Pizza §
(Serves 1)

Just right for a no-muss, no-fuss supper while you watch a favorite
TV program.

  4 biscuits from refrigerated package. (There are usually 10
    to a package—bake them all and save the extras for
    future meals).
  1/2 cup lean ground beef or pork sausage
  1 tablespoon vegetable oil
  3 tablespoons tomato sauce

Grated cheese
2 tablespoons chopped onion
1 tablespoon Mixed Herbs

Preheat oven to 400°.
Place biscuits on ungreased baking sheet. With water glass, press
  biscuits into flat circles.
Sauté ground beef and onion until lightly browned. Add herbs.
Top each biscuit with a spoonful each of tomato sauce, meat
mixture and grated cheese.
Bake 10-12 minutes.

Chewing Solutions
When chewing is a problem or dentures give you trouble:
eat a variety of softer foods (mashed potatoes, eggs, cottage
cheese, oatmeal, cream of wheat, applesauce, gelatin, banana).
Use tools for the work your teeth can't do. Grind or chop fruits,
vegetables and meats in a grinder, blender or food processor.
Your kitchen knife can help, too. Use it to chop raw foods finely
instead of serving them whole or sliced.

PORK & HAM

§ Midwest Pork Chops §
(Serves 2)

Good old-fashioned midwestern cooking makes use of regional foods, as in this succulent recipe from Fred Johnson, born and raised in Illinois farm country.

  2 pork chops
  1 tablespoon vegetable oil
  2 teaspoons chopped onion
  1/4 teaspoon sweet basil
  1/4 teaspoon thyme
  1/2 cup creamed corn
  2 tablespoons chopped green bell pepper
  1 tablespoon yogurt or cream
  2 tablespoons flour
  Dash pepper

Preheat oven to 350°.
Brown chops on both sides in oil in skillet.
Place chops in baking dish.
Mix all other ingredients and spread over chops.
Cover and bake 45 minutes.

Liquids are Important
Most people know the value of fiber in the diet, but many are not aware that with increased fiber, we need more liquids. Drink water at mealtimes and during the day—8 to 10 cups. Serve more than coffee with meals: bouillon, vegetable juice, fruit juice and soup are good choices. Plenty of non-alcoholic liquid intake will help prevent dehydration, constipation and illness.

§ Pineapple Pork Chops §
(Serves 2)

2 lean pork chops or shoulder steaks
1 tablespoon vegetable oil
1 tablespoon flour
1/2 cup canned crushed pineapple
1/4 teaspoon curry powder
1 teaspoon cornstarch
2 teaspoons brown sugar
2 teaspoons prepared mustard
1/2 cup wine or pineapple juice or water
Dash pepper

Preheat oven to 350°.
Sprinkle chops with flour, salt and pepper.
Brown chops in oil in skillet.
Place chops in baking dish.
Stir all other ingredients into skillet and simmer until slightly
thickened.
Pour sauce over chops, cover and bake 30 minutes.

§ Cranberry Pork Steaks §
(Serves 2)

Combine meaty pork with the tartness of cranberries for the best
flavors of both. Save some pork for tomorrow's dinner, or cook
an extra steak.
2 lean pork steaks
Dash pepper
2 tablespoons jellied or whole cranberry sauce, fresh or
canned
2 slices orange peel (or 1 teaspoon grated peel)

Place steaks in baking pan and sprinkle with pepper.
Top each steak with cranberry sauce and orange peel.
Bake uncovered for 45 minutes.

§ Pineapple Sweet and Sour Pork §
(Serves 2)

1/2 pound lean pork, cut into cubes
1 tablespoon vegetable oil
1/2 cup beef bouillon
Dash pepper
2 tablespoons chopped green pepper
2 tablespoons chopped green onion (scallion)
1/2 cup crushed or chunk canned pineapple
1 tablespoon sugar
1/4 cup juice from pineapple
2 tablespoons vinegar
1 tablespoon cornstarch
1 teaspoon soy sauce

Brown pork cubes in oil in skillet.
Add pepper and bouillon and simmer 30 minutes.
Add vegetables and pineapple.
Mix all other ingredients together, stir and add to pork dish.
Simmer 10 minutes, stirring.

Seek Variety

To maintain a balanced diet and fend off mealtime boredom, eat a variety of foods. Be adventurous and try a new flavor or dish or spice occasionally. Once you may have disliked cayenne pepper or yogurt or broccoli; but tastes change, and you may find new enjoyment that surprises you.

---

§ Sausage Pepper Sauté §
(Serves 2)

1/4 pound sliced pork sausage
2 tablespoons chopped onion
2 tablespoons chopped bell pepper
2 tablespoons chopped mushrooms
1 garlic clove, minced
1 tablespoon sherry (optional)
1 teaspoon Mixed Herbs
Chopped parsley

Sauté sausage pieces in skillet.
Add onions and peppers and sauté until golden brown.
Add garlic, herbs and sherry and simmer 5 minutes.
Sprinkle with parsley.

§ Curried Ham with Fruit §
(Serves 1)

Spicy and fruity, but not too sweet.
1 slice cooked ham
1/4 cup crushed pineapple with juice (or chopped peaches)
1 teaspoon lemon juice
1 teaspoon brown sugar
1/2 teaspoon curry powder

Heat oven to 350°.
Mix all ingredients except ham.
Place ham slice in baking dish or on piece of aluminum foil with
  sides turned up to form edges.
Pour sauce over ham.
Bake 15 minutes.

§ Succotash Ham §
(Serves 2)

1/2 onion, chopped
1 tablespoon butter or margarine
1/4 cup water
1/2 cup fresh or frozen lima beans
1/2 teaspoon Mixed Herbs
1 cup corn, fresh or frozen
1/2 cup diced, cooked lean ham

Sauté onions in butter in saucepan until yellow.
Add water, beans and seasonings and simmer, covered, 15 minutes.
Add corn and simmer, uncovered, 3 minutes.
Add ham cubes and heat.

§ Sugar-and-Spice Ham Loaf §
(1 small loaf)

Serve this lightly spiced ham dish hot or cold; leftovers make excellent sandwich fillings, spread with mustard or mayonnaise.

1/2 cup dry bread crumbs
1/3 cup milk
1 egg, lightly beaten
1 cup cooked ham, ground or chopped fine
1 teaspoon brown sugar
Pinch cloves
1/4 teaspoon dry mustard

Preheat oven to 350°.
Mix bread crumbs, milk and egg.
Add all other ingredients and stir gently.
Place in oiled loaf pan and bake 40 minutes.

§ Ham-Stuffed Squash §
(Serves 2)

1 acorn squash
2 tablespoons cooked lean chopped ham
2 tablespoons crushed pineapple *or* cranberry sauce
1 tablespoon brown sugar *or* 1 tablespoon orange juice

Preheat oven to 350°.
Split squash and remove seeds.
Place cut sides down on baking sheet and bake 30 minutes.
Mix all other ingredients.
Remove squash halves from oven, turn cut sides up and fill each
    with ham mixture.
Bake 30 minutes, until tender.

§ Supper Salad §
(serves 1)

1/2 cooked potato, cut in cubes
1 stalk celery, chopped
1 green onion (scallion), chopped
1/3 cup cooked, diced ham
3 tablespoons mayonnaise
1/4 teaspoon dill
1/2 teaspoon prepared mustard
1 teaspoon vinegar
Parsley

Combine potato, celery, onion, and ham.
Mix mayonnaise with dill, mustard, and vinegar.
Combine both mixtures and chill.
Garnish with parsley.

POULTRY

§ Chicken Curry §
(Serves 2)

1/2 cup cubed cooked chicken
3 tablespoons onion, chopped
3 tablespoons vegetable oil, butter or margarine
1 clove garlic, pressed or minced
3 tablespoons flour
1-1/2 cups chicken broth or bouillon
1 tablespoon curry powder
1/4 teaspoon tumeric
Dash cayenne pepper
3 tablespoons chopped apple
3 tablespoons raisins

Sauté onion in butter or oil in saucepan until golden.
Add garlic and apple, stir and remove with onion from pan. Set
aside.
Stir flour and seasonings into hot oil and cook until bubbly.
Add broth, stirring until thick.
Add chicken, cooked onion mixture and raisins, and heat.
Serve with condiments such as coconut, chopped banana, peanuts
  and chutney.

Almost-Free Soup
Save the bones of poultry, meat or fish in a plastic bag in the
refrigerator (or freezer, if saving longer than 2 days). When
you've collected a few odds and ends of vegetables—half an
onion here, a zucchini there—throw them together with 3 cups
of water, parsley sprigs, a bay leaf, a squeeze of lemon, a garlic
clove, and a dash of salt and pepper. Simmer for a couple of
hours, discard the bones, and you'll have a nutritious, delicious
meal that costs next to nothing.

§ Mustard Cream Chicken §
(Serves 2)

Dale Welton retired engineer, likes the tangy touch of mustard in this chicken dish, his kitchen specialty. "It not only tastes great, it's low in fat," he says.

3 - 4 chicken pieces, skin removed.
3 tablespoons Dijon-style mustard
1/4 teaspoon pepper
1/2 cup chicken broth or bouillon
1/3 cup yogurt

Spread mustard over chicken pieces and refrigerate 3 or more hours.
Preheat oven to 350°.
Place chicken pieces in baking dish and sprinkle with pepper.
Add chicken broth.
Bake 40 minutes, basting occasionally.
Remove from oven and stir in yogurt.
Return to oven and heat for 5 minutes.

§ Chicken Cacciatore §
(Serves 1-2)

2 -3 pieces chicken, skin removed
1 tablespoon vegetable oil
1 clove garlic, pressed or minced
1/2 teaspoon rosemary
2 tablespoons vinegar
1/2 cup red wine
1/4 teaspoon pepper
2 tablespoons tomato paste
3 tablespoons chicken broth or bouillon

Sauté chicken pieces in oil in skillet until lightly browned.
Add garlic and stir.
Add rosemary, vinegar, pepper and wine. Simmer, uncovered, to
reduce liquid.
Add tomato paste and broth, or tomato sauce, and simmer 30
minutes, turning chicken pieces occasionally.

§ Chicken Salad §
(Serves 2)

1/2 cup cubed cooked chicken
1 celery stalk, chopped
1 teaspoon lemon juice
3 tablespoons mayonnaise
1/4 teaspoon tarragon
Dash salt and pepper
1 hardcooked egg, cut in chunks
2 tablespoons chopped almonds or other nuts
Lettuce

Toss together all ingredients except egg, nuts and lettuce.
Fold in eggs and chill.
Arrange on lettuce leaves and sprinkle with nuts.

Spices versus Digestion

When you're trying to lower salt intake but find certain herbs
and spices upsetting, it's hard to avoid a bland, flavorless diet.
One answer: Experiment. If you can't tolerate one spice, try
another or try smaller quantities. Keep experimenting until you find what suits you and your digestion.

§ Chicken a' la King §
(Serves 2)

1 tablespoon butter or margarine
1/4 cup chopped celery
1 tablespoon chopped green pepper
1 tablespoon flour
1/2 teaspoon Mixed Herbs
1 cup chicken broth or bouillon
1/2 cup cooked cubed chicken
1/4 cup evaporated milk

Sauté celery and green pepper in butter in saucepan.
Stir in flour and herbs.
Add chicken broth and stir until thickened.
Add chicken and milk and heat to simmer.

§ Baked Chicken §
(Serves 1)

Versatile chicken is here popped into the oven and left to turn brown and tender. Save the bones for delicious homemade soup.

2 pieces chicken, with skin removed.
1 tablespoon vegetable oil
1 teaspoon butter or margarine
1/4 teaspoon Mixed Herbs
Dash pepper
1 garlic clove, pressed or minced
2 tablespoons lemon juice
1 tablespoon honey

Preheat oven to 350°.
Heat butter and oil in baking pan in oven until butter melts.
Sprinkle chicken pieces with herbs and pepper.
Dip each chicken piece in melted butter and oil and turn.
Bake 40 minutes.
Mix garlic, lemon juice, and honey in bowl.
Pour over chicken and return dish to oven for 10-15 minutes.

§ Ginger-Coconut Chicken §
(Serves 1-2)

2 pieces chicken with skin removed
1 tablespoon vegetable oil
2 tablespoons plain yogurt
1 tablespoon prepared mustard
2 tablespoons chopped or flaked coconut
1/2 teaspoon chopped fresh ginger
Dash salt

Heat oil in skillet.
Sauté chicken pieces until golden brown.
Pour off excess fat, cover, and cook over low heat 20 minutes.
Mix yogurt, mustard, ginger and salt and pour over chicken.
Continue cooking, uncovered, 5 minutes.
Sprinkle with coconut before serving.

Drugs and Alcohol
If you're on medication, avoid alcohol. It can be dangerous to your health to mix tranquilizers, painkillers, antibiotics, antihistamines or other drugs with alcohol. Don't drink while you're taking drugs without your doctor's specific approval.

§ Chicken With Greens and Tomato §
(Serves 2)

3 - 4 pieces chicken
2 tablespoons butter or vegetable oil
1 clove garlic, minced or pressed
1 green onion (scallion), chopped
1/2 green bell pepper, chopped
2 tablespoons chopped parsley
1/2 teaspoon Mixed Herbs
1/2 cup fresh or canned tomatoes, chopped

Preheat oven to 350°.
Sauté chicken in butter or oil in skillet until browned.
Place chicken in baking dish.
Add all other ingredients.
Cover and bake 40 minutes. If sauce is too thin, thicken with flour.

§ Chicken Liver Special §
(Serves 2)

1/4 pound chicken livers
1/2 onion, chopped
1 tablespoon vegetable oil
1/4 cup chicken broth or bouillon
1/4 teaspoon fresh chopped ginger
1/4 teaspoon sugar
1/4 teaspoon lemon juice

Sauté onion in hot oil until yellow.
Add livers and sauté 5 minutes.
Add all other ingredients and simmer 5 minutes. If sauce is too
  thin, thicken with 1 teaspoon cornstarch dissolved in water.

§ Stir-Fried Chicken §
(Serves 2)

1/2 cup chopped broccoli
2 tablespoons vegetable oil
1 garlic clove, minced
1/2 teaspoon fresh ginger, minced
2 tablespoons bean sprouts, fresh or canned
2 tablespoons water chestnut, sliced
1/4 cup snow peas (optional)
1/2 cup chicken broth or water
1 tablespoon soy sauce
1 cup cooked chicken, cut in strips

Heat vegetable oil in skillet or wok.
Add broccoli and cook, stirring, until bright green—about 3
  minutes.
Stir in garlic and ginger.
Add all other ingredients and cook, stirring, until heated through.

Vinegar, The Kitchen Helper

Lowly, inexpensive vinegar can be used in many ways other than cooking. Use it (2 or 3 tablespoons) when washing dishes, along with your regular detergent, to make dishes shine. Rinse jars for food storage with a mixture of water and vinegar, to eliminate odor. Clean appliances and countertops with full-strength vinegar to cut through grease and grime. Wipe the rubber tubing on the refrigerator door, as well as the refrigerator interior, with vinegar; this helps prevent mildew. Freshen your coffeemaker by running it through a cycle with vinegar and water—then rinse. Use full-strength vinegar to remove fruit and vegetable stains from fingers and dishes.

§ Stuffed Cornish Game Hen §
(Serves 2)

1 game hen (thaw if frozen)
1/2 onion cut in small chunks
1/2 celery stalk in chunks
Juice of 1/4 lemon
1/2 teaspoon Mixed Herbs
2 tablespoons melted butter

Preheat oven to 350°.
Place hen in small roasting pan.
Pour lemon juice into hen.
Stuff hen with onion, celery, herbs and squeezed lemon section.
Drizzle with melted butter.
Roast one hour, basting occasionally with pan juices.

§ Sweet and Sour Chicken §
(Serves 1-2)

2 pieces chicken, skin removed
2 tablespoons prepared mustard
2 tablespoons honey
2 tablespoons lemon juice
1 teaspoon soy sauce
1 teaspoon vinegar

Combine all ingredients in bowl.
Marinate in refrigerator for 1-2 hours.
Place chicken pieces on broiling pan.
Broil 10 minutes, basting with sauce occasionally.
Turn pieces and broil another 10 minutes.

§ Chicken Milano §

(Serves 2)

1 cup cooked chicken, cubed
1 tablespoon vegetable oil, butter or margarine
2 tablespoons chopped onion
1 tablespoon flour
Dash pepper
1 clove garlic, minced or pressed
1/4 teaspoon salt
1 cup chicken broth or bouillon
2 tablespoons peas, fresh or frozen
1 tablespoon sherry (optional)
2 tablespoons grated Parmesan cheese
1 cup cooked brown rice

Melt butter in saucepan.
Sauté onion and garlic in butter until golden (do not brown).
Add salt, pepper and flour and stir until bubbly.
Add broth and simmer, stirring, until mixture thickens.
Add peas, cover and simmer 5 minutes.
Add chicken and sherry and heat.
Spoon over rice and sprinkle with cheese.

Enjoy Every Mouthful
Eating well involves more than providing fuel for your body. It's a sensory experience meant to be savored. Eat slowly, taking the time to appreciate and enjoy your meal.

§ Salad Dressing Chicken §
(Serves 1-2)

2 pieces chicken, skinned
2 tablespoons oil-and-vinegar salad dressing
1 tablespoon vegetable oil

Coat chicken pieces with dressing.
Place in refrigerator 3-6 hours.
Sauté chicken in oil in skillet until browned.
Cover and continue cooking over low heat 30 minutes.

§ Tarragon Chicken §
(Serves 2)

4 pieces chicken
2 tablespoons butter, margarine, or vegetable oil
2 tablespoons flour
1/4 teaspoon salt
1/8 teaspoon pepper
1/8 teaspoon paprika
1/4 teaspoon tarragon

Preheat oven to 400°.
Melt butter or oil in baking pan in oven.
Mix flour and herbs in bowl.
Dip chicken pieces in flour mixture, covering all sides.
Place chicken in single layer in baking pan.
Bake 30 minutes. Turn chicken pieces and continue baking 20
   minutes, until tender. For crisp skin, broil 3-4 minutes after
   chicken is cooked.

§ Chicken Parmesan §
(Serves 1-2)

2 pieces chicken, skin removed
1/2 cup soft bread crumbs
1/4 cup grated Parmesan cheese
1 clove garlic, pressed or minced
1/4 teaspoon salt (1/2 teaspoon garlic salt may be
   substituted and garlic omitted)
Dash pepper
2 tablespoons vegetable oil or melted butter

Preheat oven to 350°.
Mix all ingredients except chicken and oil or butter in bowl.
Dip chicken pieces in oil or butter, then in crumb mixture, coating
   well
Place chicken in single layer in baking pan.
Pour any remaining butter or oil over chicken.
Bake 1 hour.

§ Fruit Juice Chicken §
(Serves 2)

As the chicken bakes, the fruit juices bubble around it, creating
a sauce that is tangy, with a hint of sweetness—a perfect complement to tender, moist chicken.

2 chicken breast halves, with skin removed
1 tablespoon melted butter or margarine
1/4 teaspoon salt
1/8 teaspoon pepper
1/2 teaspoon fresh chopped ginger (optional)
1/2 cup grapefruit juice
1/2 cup pineapple juice

Preheat oven to 350°.
Place chicken breasts in baking pan.
Pour butter over and sprinkle with salt and pepper.
Pour juices over chicken.
Add ginger.
Bake 45 minutes.

§ Jambalaya Chicken §
(Serves 2 with leftovers)

1 tablespoon vegetable oil
1 stalk celery, chopped
1/4 cup chopped onion
1/4 cup chopped green pepper
1/2 cup uncooked white rice
1 cup chicken broth or bouillon
1 clove garlic, chopped or pressed
Dash cayenne pepper
1 cup cooked chicken, cut in cubes

Sauté celery, onion and green pepper in oil in skillet until lightly
browned.
Add all other ingredients except chicken.
Cover and simmer 20 minutes, until rice is tender.
Stir in chicken and simmer 5 minutes.

Be Sociable

Mealtime is a social time. You'll enjoy eating far more if you
have company. Invite a neighbor or friend to join you for dinner. Share a potluck with a neighbor. Cultivate new and old
acquaintances and keep your zest for food and friends alive.

§ Chicken-Stuffed Tomato §
(Serves 1)

1/3 cup diced, cooked chicken
2 teaspoons mayonnaise
1 teaspoon lemon juice
1 teaspoon chopped parsley
1/2 celery stalk, chopped
1 tablespoon chopped water chestnuts (optional)
1 fresh tomato
Lettuce

Combine all ingredients except tomato and lettuce.
Slice top from tomato and scoop out seeds and flesh, leaving thick shell.
Chop tomato flesh and add to chicken mixture.
Spoon into tomato shell and serve on lettuce.

§ Chicken Cobbler §
(Serves 1)

1/3 cup cooked, diced chicken
1 cup chicken broth or bouillon
1 tablespoon flour mixed smooth in 1/4 cup water
2 tablespoons frozen peas
1/4 teaspoon salt
1/4 teaspoon Mixed Herbs
2 biscuits, uncooked (packaged refrigerated or homemade)

Preheat oven to 400°.
Mix all ingredients except biscuits.
Pour into baking dish or pie pan.
Flatten biscuits slightly and place on chicken mixture.
Bake 15 minutes, until biscuits are golden brown.

§ Penny's Thousand-Year Chicken Soup §

Penny Avila, a gifted and well-known poet, says she has been cooking this delicious soup for "a thousand years." Her family and guests still love it. Refrigerate or freeze the unused portion for another meal.

Back and neck of chicken or turkey
2 whole onions, cut in chunks
2 stalks celery, cut in chunks
1 parsnip, chopped
1 turnip, chopped
2 carrots, sliced
1/2 teaspoon salt
Water

Pull and discard fat and skin from poultry.
Place chicken pieces in kettle and cover completely with water.
Bring to a boil and skim off foam.
Add all other ingredients.
Simmer 3 hours.
Discard bones before serving.

Freezer and Microwave: If You've Got Them, Use Them

Two conveniences that make life in the kitchen easier are the freezer and microwave oven. If you have either or both of these appliances, take advantage of them. Buy ground beef or chops in volume and freeze serving-size quantities. When you make soup, double the quantity and freeze half of it. Frozen foods thaw swiftly and cooking time is cut drastically with a microwave oven.

§ Turkey Parmesan §
(Serves 2)

1/2 pound ground turkey or 1 cup finely-chopped, cooked
   turkey
1 egg, lightly beaten
1/4 cup dry bread or cracker crumbs
1 tablespoon Italian-style salad dressing (or other favorite
   style)
Dash pepper
1 tablespoon vegetable oil
2 tablespoons tomato sauce
1/4 teaspoon sweet basil
2 tablespoons grated Parmesan cheese

Mix turkey with egg, crumbs, salad dressing and pepper and form
   patties.
Heat oil in skillet and brown patties on both sides.
Sprinkle tomato sauce on patties.
Sprinkle each patty with sweet basil and cheese.
Serve or broil 1 minute to melt cheese.

§ Turkey Tetrazzini §
(Serves 2)

4 ounces spaghetti, cooked
1/2 cup cooked, diced turkey
1/4 cup fresh mushrooms, chopped
2 tablespoons butter or margarine
1 tablespoon flour
1/2 cup turkey or chicken broth or bouillon
1/3 cup milk
1 tablespoon sherry (optional)

1/4 teaspoon sage
Dash salt and pepper
2 tablespoons grated Parmesan cheese

Preheat oven to 325°.
Melt butter in saucepan.
Sauté mushrooms and remove from butter
Stir flour into butter and heat until mixture bubbles.
Add broth and stir over low heat until thickened.
Add milk, sherry and seasonings.
Stir in turkey, mushrooms and cooked spaghetti.
Place mixture in baking dish and top with cheese.
Bake uncovered 15 minutes, until golden brown.

§ Turkey Patties §
(Serves 2)

1/2 pound ground turkey
1/2 teaspoon sage
1 tablespoon chopped onion
Dash salt and pepper
1 tablespoon vegetable oil

Mix all ingredients except oil.
Form patties.
Sauté oil in skillet 8 minutes on each side.

Buy Small
Buy only what you need, to avoid needless waste and expense.
Unless you plan to use that extra cup of canned corn within
a day or two, it's better to buy the smaller sized can. Other-
wise it will probably sit in your refrigerator until it's too old
to use.

§ Lo-Cal Turkey Breast §
(Serves 2, with leftovers)

Crisp on the outside, moist inside—without skin or salt.

Turkey breast (thaw if frozen)
1 cup water
1 clove garlic, minced
1 tablespoon chopped onion
1/4 teaspoon nutmeg
1/2 teaspoon Mixed Herbs
1/8 teaspoon sage
1/8 teaspoon pepper
1/8 teaspoon paprika

Heat oven to 350°.
Remove turkey skin.
Place turkey breast on rack in baking dish or roasting pan.
Pour water into pan (pan should be half-filled with water).
Sprinkle turkey with all other ingredients.
Bake 20 minutes per pound of turkey.

§ Turkey with Broccoli and Almonds §
(Serves 2)

Rosemary Webster finds this a flavorsome way to make use of left-over turkey. It's quick to fix and goes well with potatoes or yams. Serve it with a crisp green salad, and you have a fine meal.

1 cup cut-up cooked turkey or 3/4 cup ground cooked turkey
1/2 can (11-1/2 ounce size) cream of mushroom soup
1/4 cup water or chicken or turkey broth

1 tablespoon sherry (optional)
1/2 cup cut-up fresh or frozen broccoli pieces
2 tablespoons chopped almonds

Preheat oven to 400°.
Mix all ingredients except almonds.
Place in baking dish and bake 20 minutes.
Sprinkle with almonds.

Losing Weight

If you are heavier than your ideal weight, consult your doctor or dietitian and plan a weight-loss diet. If you exercise, eat wisely, and cut down on fats and sugar, the extra pounds will melt away. A few tips for losing weight:
—Don't skip meals. Eat three small meals a day and snack on low-calorie foods such as carrots, celery and fruits.
—Eat fish and poultry more frequently than red meat.
—Keep busy; don't eat out of boredom.
—Don't deprive yourself. With your doctor or dietitian work out a diet that includes your favorite foods.
—Avoid alcohol; drink plenty of water and fruit juices.

SEAFOOD

§ Fish Fillet Vinaigrette §
(Serves 2)

A low-sodium, low-cholesterol dish that gives a tangy boost to nutritious seafood. The sauce does double-duty: any leftover vinaigrette not cooked with the fish may be used as salad dressing!

  2 fish fillets, fresh or frozen and thawed
  1 tablespoon vinegar
  2 tablespoons vegetable oil
  1/4 teaspoon crumbled dry tarragon or 1/2 teaspoon fresh
    tarragon
  1/8 teaspoon black pepper
  Pinch paprika
  2 tablespoons grated Parmesan or Swiss cheese (optional)

Heat oven to 400°.
Mix vinegar, oil tarragon, pepper and paprika to make vinaigrette.
Place 1 tablespoon vinaigrette in baking dish.
Place fillets in baking dish.
Spoon sauce over fillets until coated.
Bake 12 minutes, until fish is tender and flakes easily.
Sprinkle with grated cheese; return to oven to melt cheese.

Fish Oil

Remember the old-fashioned tonic, cod-liver oil? Scientists are finding the Grandma was right: Oil from fish may not have nutritional value, but supply substances that reduce blood pressure, lower cholesterol, and protect against some diseases. To get the benefits of "omega-3" fatty acids, many nutritionists recommend eating fish two or three times a week. Large quantities, such as those found in fish-oil capsules, are not necessary.

§ Fish Special §
(Serves 2)

1/2 pound white fish (halibut, snapper, cod, perch)
1/2 cup chopped onion
1 clove garlic, minced
2 tablespoons chopped mushrooms
1 tablespoon butter
1/2 cup spinach, fresh or frozen and thawed
1/2 teaspoon salt
Dash pepper
1 egg
1 tablespoon grated Parmesan cheese

Place fish in skillet of simmering water with slice of onion and
 lemon.
Cover and simmer 5-7 minutes.
Drain, remove fish from pan and flake with fork, discarding skin
 and bones.
Sauté onion, garlic and mushrooms in butter in skillet.
Add fish, spinach and seasoning and simmer 4 minutes.
Add egg and stir.
When egg is set, sprinkle with cheese.

§ Fish With Herbs §
(Serves 2)

1/2 pound fish fillets
1 tablespoon butter or margarine
2 tablespoons chopped onion
Dash salt
1 teaspoon Mixed Herbs
2 teaspoons lemon juice

1 teaspoon cornstarch
1/4 cup white wine or chicken or fish broth
1 egg yolk
1 tablespoon chopped nuts (optional)

Preheat oven to 400°.
Sauté fish fillets and onion in butter for 3 minutes, turning fish once.
Mix together lemon juice, cornstarch, wine and egg in saucepan and cook until thickened. Add herbs.
Place fish in baking dish and pour sauce over.
Bake until sauce bubbles, about 10 minutes.
Garnish with minced parsely.

§ Fish in Mushroom Cream Sauce §
(Serves 2)

1/2 pound fish fillets (any firm, white fish)
2 tablespoons butter or margarine
1/2 onion, chopped
1/2 cup chopped mushrooms
1 tablespoon lemon juice
1/2 teaspoon teriyaki or Worcestershire sauce
1/2 teaspoon prepared mustard
1/2 cup plain yogurt

Sauté onions and mushrooms in butter in skillet until lightly browned, and remove from pan. Set aside.
Cut fish into bite-sized pieces.
Sauté fish pieces in butter until golden brown.
Add onions, mushrooms and all other ingredients.
Stir and heat until mixture bubbles.

§ Dilly Yogurt Fish §
(Serves 2)

1/2 pound frozen fish fillets
1/4 cup dry white wine
1/2 chicken bouillon cube with 2 tablespoons water
   or 2 tablespoons chicken broth
1/4 teaspoon dill
Dash pepper
2 tablespoons plain yogurt

Place fillets in baking dish.
Pour all ingredients except yogurt over fillets.
Cover and leave to thaw at room temperature.
Preheat oven to 350°.
When fish fillets are thawed, bake 20 minutes, basting occasionally.
Drain liquid from cooked fish into saucepan and simmer until it
   reduces to about 1/3 cup. (For additional flavor, add a spoonful
   of chopped mushrooms and onions.)
Stir in yogurt and heat. Serve sauce over fish.

Accessorize

Just as a touch of jewelry adds interest to clothing, so "accessories" add interest to food. The possibilities are endless.
Try these, for example:
—chopped nuts on cooked broccoli
—cinnamon on yogurt
—dash of hot pepper sauce in tomato juice
—chopped chives over scrambled eggs
—mint leaves in cucumber salad
—chili powder in split-pea soup
—crushed ginger snap cookies on fruit

§ Spicy Red Snapper §
(Serves 2)

1/2 pound red snapper
2 tablespoons Worcestershire or steak sauce
1 tablespoon catsup
1 tablespoon vegetable oil
1 teaspoon vinegar
1/4 teaspoon curry

Cut fish into bite-sized pieces and place in greased baking pan.
Combine all other ingredients and pour over fish.
Broil 3 inches from heat for 4 minutes.
Turn and brush with sauce.
Broil 4 minutes longer, until fish is tender.

§ Ginger Snapper §
(Serves 2)

Not the cookie variety, but a well-seasoned, gingery red snapper, its sauce an excellent complement to the nutritious fish.

1/2 pound red snapper fillet
1/4 teaspoon pepper
1 tablespoon vegetable oil
2 tablespoons chopped onion
1 clove garlic, chopped or pressed
1 teaspoon chopped fresh ginger
2 tablespoons sherry or white wine

Cut fish into strips or bite-sized pieces and sprinkle with pepper.
Sauté onion in oil in skillet until lightly browned.
Remove onion and set aside.

Sauté fish until golden brown.
Stir in ginger and garlic.
Add wine and simmer 5-8 minutes, until fish flakes easily with
    fork.

§ Baked Fish With Mushrooms and Tomato §
(Serves 2)

1/2 pound white fish fillets
2 tablespoons lemon juice
1 sliced tomato
1/2 cup sliced mushrooms, fresh or canned, and drained
1/2 teaspoon Mixed Herbs
1/2 onion, chopped
1 tablespoon vegetable oil or butter

Preheat oven to 350°.
Place fish fillets in baking dish and pour lemon juice over.
Add tomato slices, mushrooms, herbs and onion.
Drizzle with oil or butter.
Cover and bake 10 minutes.
Uncover and bake 10 more minutes.

Lemon, the Great Flavorizer
Many good cooks say their secret lies in that package of tangy
flavor, the lemon. Its juice and grated rind can enhance almost
any dish, from meat loaf to oatmeal cookies. To make a lemon
easier to squeeze, simmer the whole fruit in water for 5 minutes.

§ Foil Fish §
(Serves 1)

1 fillet of firm-fleshed white fish
1/2 lemon, sliced
1 tablespoon melted butter
1 tablespoon white wine, sherry or chicken broth
Dash salt and pepper

Preheat oven to 375°.
Place fish on sheet of aluminum foil.
Place lemon slices over.
Add other ingredients and fold edges of foil tightly over.
Bake 15 minutes.

§ Spicy Fish Stew §
(Serves 2)

1 cup (one 8 ounce can) stewed tomatoes with liquid
   (Cajun-style is best)
1/4 cup water
1 small potato, chopped
1/2 cup chopped celery
1/2 cup chopped onion
1/2 pound firm-fleshed white fish, cut in bite-sized pieces
1/4 teaspoon Mixed Hot Spices

Place tomatoes, liquid and water in saucepan and bring to boil.
Add potatoes, cover and cook until nearly tender (about 8 minutes).
Add all other ingredients, cover and simmer 10 minutes.

§ Curried Fish Bites §
(Serves 2)

1/2 pound white fish fillet, cut in bite-sized pieces
2 tablespoons flour
1 tablespoon wheat germ
1 teaspoon curry
Dash cayenne
2 tablespoons vegetable oil
1 tablespoon butter or margarine
1/4 cup chopped nuts
Parsley

Mix flour with seasonings.
Coat fish pieces with flour mixture.
Heat oil and butter in skillet.
Sauté fish until lightly browned on all sides, about 10 minutes.
Sprinkle nuts on fish and garnish with parsley.

§ Fish On Spinach §
(Serves 2)

1/2 pound white fish fillets
1 tablespoon lemon juice
1 cup chopped spinach, fresh or frozen and thawed
1 tablespoon vegetable oil
Dash salt and pepper
1/4 teaspoon nutmeg
2 tablespoons grated Swiss cheese

Preheat oven to 350°.
Sauté fish in oil in skillet until lightly browned.
Place spinach in buttered baking dish.

Place fish on spinach bed.
Sprinkle with seasonings and cheese.
Bake 15 minutes.

§ Fish-Stuffed Peppers §
(Serves 2)

2 green bell peppers
1/2 cup cooked fish, flaked
1/4 cup chopped onion
1/4 cup bread crumbs
1 tablespoon lemon juice
1/4 teaspoon salt
Dash pepper
1/4 cup tomato sauce
1/4 teaspoon dill

Preheat oven to 350°.
Cut tops from peppers and remove seeds and membranes.
Blanch peppers for 3 minutes in simmering water in saucepan.
Mix fish, onion, crumbs, lemon juice, salt and pepper.
Add dill to tomato sauce.
Stuff peppers with fish mixture and place in baking dish.
Pour sauce over.
Bake 20 minutes.

Grow and Snip Your Own
Fresh herbs add sparkle and verve to your meals, and the best way to get them is to grow your own. If you don't have outdoor space, grow chives, marjoram and thyme in pots on your kitchen windowsill. (Don't overwater, or they'll be spindly.) When you want a spoonful, all you do is snip!

§ Salmon With Cheese §
(Serves 2)

Good as a casserole or spread, hot or cold, on crackers or toast.

1 tablespoon butter or margarine
1 tablespoon flour
1/2 cup canned salmon
Liquid from salmon and water to equal 1/2 cup
1/4 teaspoon dill
2 tablespoons bread crumbs, buttered
2 tablespoons grated cheese

Preheat oven to 400°.
Melt butter in saucepan.
Stir in flour, salt and pepper, and heat until bubbly.
Add liquid and stir until thick.
Add salmon.
Place mixture in baking dish or custard cups.
Top with bread crumbs and cheese.
Bake 15 minutes.

§ Salmon Steaks Superb §
(Serves 2)

2 fresh salmon steaks
1/4 cup sliced fresh mushrooms
1 tablespoon butter or margarine
1/4 cup white wine
Dash salt and pepper
Hollandaise Sauce (page 85)

Sauté mushrooms in butter in skillet. Remove mushrooms from
  pan and set aside.
Sauté salmon lightly (add more butter if necessary).
Add wine, seasonings and mushrooms and simmer 10 minutes.
Serve with warm Hollandaise Sauce.

§ Tasty Tuna §
(Serves 1)

Simple to prepare, yet packed with protein, vitamins, and flavor.

  1/2 cup canned tuna fish
  1/3 cup cracker crumbs
  1 tablespoon chopped onion
  2 tablespoons chopped celery
  1 tablespoon mayonnaise, sour cream, or yogurt
  1/8 teaspoon pepper
  Slice of cheddar or Swiss cheese

Preheat oven to 325°.
Mix all ingredients except cheese in baking dish.
Top with cheese.
Bake 20 minutes.

§ Tuna Chowder §
(Serves 2)

  2 tablespoons dry onion soup mix
  2 cups water
  Dash pepper
  Dash cayenne
  2 stalks celery, chopped
  1/2 cup noodles

1 6-1/4 ounce can water-packed tuna
2 tablespoons frozen peas
1 egg yolk
1/2 cup light cream or milk

Combine soup mix and water and bring to boil in saucepan.
Add seasonings, celery, and noodles.
Cook uncovered 10 minutes.
Stir in tuna and peas and simmer 15 minutes.
Beat egg yolk with cream or milk and stir mixture into chowder.
Heat and serve.

§ Tuna-Vegie Dish §
(Serves 2, with leftovers)

1 celery stalk, sliced
1/2 tablespoon chopped onion
1/2 cup water
1/2 teaspoon Mixed Herbs
1 cup canned tomatoes
1/2 cup uncooked brown or white rice
1 can tuna fish, drained

Mix celery, onion, water, herbs and tomato liquid in skillet and
   bring to boil.
Add rice and bring to boil.
Cover and simmer 20 minutes for white rice, 45 minutes for brown.
Add tomatoes and tuna and heat.

§ Tuna Loaf §
(Serves 2)

Protein-rich, low in fat, and inexpensive, this loaf recipe was developed by Jacquelyn Bee, an energetic 82-year-old. She serves it with lemon wedges, green beans, and a mixed-fruit salad.

1/2 cup water-packed tuna fish, drained
2 tablespoons dry bread crumbs
1 egg, slightly beaten
1 tablespoon oats
2 tablespoons skim milk
1 tablespoon lemon juice
1 tablespoon chopped parsley
1 tablespoon chopped green onion (scallion)
1/4 teaspoon salt
Dash pepper
3 tablespoons soft bread crumbs

Preheat oven to 400°.
Mix all ingredients except soft bread crumbs.
Spoon into oiled loaf pan.
Bake for 20 minutes.
Sprinkle soft crumbs over loaf and return to oven for five minutes to brown, or brown under broiler.

§ Tuna on a Muffin §
(Serves 2)

1/2 can tuna fish, drained
2 tablespoons chopped celery
2 tablespoons chopped green or dry onion
1 tablespoon chopped dill pickle or 1/4 teaspoon dill
2 teaspoons prepared mustard

2 tablespoons mayonnaise
Dash salt and pepper
3 tablespoons grated cheddar cheese

Mix all ingredients except cheese.
Spoon on English muffins and sprinkle with cheese.
Broil until cheese melts.

§ Tuna au Gratin §
(Serves 2)

1 7-ounce can tuna fish, drained
4 tablespoons chopped onion
2 tablespoons chopped green pepper
1/4 cup mayonnaise
2 tablespoons dry bread or cracker crumbs
2 tablespoons grated Parmesan or other cheese

Preheat oven to 350°.
Mix all ingredients except crumbs and cheese.
Spoon into baking dish.
Top with crumbs and cheese.
Bake 20 minutes.

§ Shrimp-Corn Curry §
(Serves 2)

1/2 cup small cooked shrimp, canned or fresh
1 cup cooked corn
1/2 cup chopped celery
1/2 teaspoon curry powder
2 tablespoons mayonnaise

Dash salt and pepper
Lettuce

Mix all ingredients.
Place in refrigerator to chill.
Serve on bed of chopped lettuce.

Drugs and Food

When you have to take medication, be aware of how drugs interact with foods. What you eat has an effect on the way drugs behave in your body, and some drugs may promote dietary deficiencies. Three popular drugs, antacids, aspirin and laxatives, are examples. The aluminum hydroxide in antacids can contribute to phosphate deficiency. Aspirin can cause bleeding in the gastrointestinal tract. Laxatives can affect the absorption of vitamin D or deplete bone phosphorus. If you take lots of aspirin to ease arthritis pain, for example, you may need a diet higher in iron and should consult your doctor about it.

EGGS & CHEESE

★ ★ ★ ★ ★

NOTE: Most physicians recommend limiting the consumption of eggs to 2 or 3 per week. Consult your doctor if you need to restrict your dietary intake of fats and/or cholesterol.

★ ★ ★ ★ ★

§ Pineapple Eggnog §
(Serves 1)

A chilled, fruit-sweetened eggnog is a winning choice for a quick dose of flavor and nutrition. Vary the fruit juices for an occasional change.

1 cup cold milk
1 egg
1 teaspoon sugar
1 teaspoon vanilla
2 tablespoons frozen concentrated pineapple or other
fruit juice
Nutmeg

Place all ingredients except nutmeg in blender or food processor and blend until smooth.
Pour into glass and sprinkle with nutmeg.

Calcium in Your Diet

Dairy products are the best source of calcium, but they may not give all you need.If your doctor suggests calcium supplements, ask about the best quantity for you. Megadoses of calcium can increase the risk of kidney stones. (A man over the age of 51 should have 1000 milligrams of calcium a day; a woman needs 1500 milligrams a day.)

§ Macaroni and Cheese §
(Serves 2)

A rich, creamy, cheesy version of an old favorite. To add even more protein, stir in cubes of cooked chicken, turkey or ham or sliced frankfurters. For lower sodium content, use chicken or turkey, low-sodium cheese, and no additional salt.

1 cup cooked macaroni noodles
1 tablespoon butter or margarine
1 tablespoon flour
1 teaspoon dry mustard
Dash hot pepper sauce
1/4 teaspoon salt
1 cup milk
1 cup grated cheddar cheese

Preheat oven to 375°.
Melt butter in saucepan.
Stir in flour, mustard and salt and heat until bubbly.
Stir in milk and cook, stirring, until slightly thickened.
Remove from heat and stir in 3/4 cup cheese and hot pepper sauce.
Add macaroni and mix.
Spoon into greased baking dish and sprinkle with remaining cheese.
Bake 20 minutes.

§ Onion-Pepper Omelet §
(Serves 1)

1/4 onion, sliced thin
1/4 green bell pepper, sliced thin
1 tablespoon vegetable oil
2 eggs
1/8 teaspoon nutmeg
1/8 teaspoon sweet basil
Dash dill, salt and pepper

Heat oil in skillet.

Sauté onion and pepper slices until onion is golden brown.

Beat eggs lightly with fork or whisk and add seasonings.

Pour into skillet and cook over medium heat until eggs are set.

Lift edges occasionally to allow uncooked portion to pour into
  bottom of pan.

With spatula, fold omelet in half. Garnish with parsley.

§ Swiss Eggs §
(Serves 1)

1 hardcooked egg, sliced
1 tablespoon butter or margarine
2 teaspoons flour
3/4 cup milk
1/4 cup grated Swiss cheese
1/4 teaspoon dry mustard
1 tablespoon sherry (optional)
1 slice toast

Preheat oven to 350°.

Melt butter in saucepan.

Stir in flour and heat until bubbly.

Slowly add milk, stirring until smooth.

Add mustard and 2 tablespoons cheese.

Add sherry.

Tear toast into bite-sized pieces and place in buttered baking dish.

Place egg slices on toast, pour sauce over and sprinkle with remaining
  cheese.

Bake 10 minutes.

§ Tomato-Egg Bake §
(Serves 1)

1 large, fresh tomato
1 egg
1/4 teaspoon dill
1 teaspoon chopped onion
1 tablespoon grated cheese (any kind)

Preheat oven to 350°.
Slice top off tomato and scoop out pulp, leaving a thick shell.
Mix tomato pulp with egg and all other ingredients.
Stuff tomato shell with mixture.
Place in buttered baking dish and bake 15 minutes.
Top with additional grated cheese and return to oven to allow cheese to melt.

§ Broccoli and Egg §
(Serves 1)

1 tablespoon vegetable oil
1/2 cup chopped fresh broccoli
1/4 cup water
1 egg
Dash salt and pepper
1/4 teaspoon sweet basil
Pinch marjoram
2 tablespoons milk

Heat oil in skillet.
Add broccoli and stir for 1 minute.
Add water, cover and simmer for 5 minutes. Remove pan from heat.

Mix egg with all other ingredients.
Pour egg mixture over broccoli and cook over low heat until egg
is set—about 4 minutes.

§ Corn Pudding §
(Serves 2)

2 eggs, beaten
1 cup cooked or canned corn, drained
1 cup milk
Dash salt
Dash hot pepper sauce
2 tablespoons chopped green onion
1 celery stalk, chopped
1 tablespoon chopped green pepper

Preheat oven to 350°.
Mix corn, eggs and milk.
Add remaining ingredients and mix.
Pour into buttered baking dish.
Set dish in hot water in shallow pan.
Bake 40 minutes, until knife inserted in center comes out clean.
Let stand 5 minutes to set before serving.

Freeze Extra Eggs
If you have more fresh eggs than you will use within ten days
or so, break them into a glass or plastic container and place
them in the freezer. They will keep for weeks. (Don't try to
freeze eggs in the shell.)

§ Mushroom-Zucchini Frittata §
(Serves 2)

1/4 cup chopped fresh or canned mushrooms
2 tablespoons chopped onion
1/4 cup chopped zucchini
2 tablespoons vegetable oil
1 clove garlic, pressed or minced
3 eggs
1/4 cup milk or cream
Dash salt and pepper
1/2 cup soft bread crumbs
1/2 cup grated cheddar cheese

Preheat oven to 350°.
Sauté mushrooms, onion and zucchini in oil in skillet until golden
  brown.
Add garlic and stir.
Beat eggs with milk or cream, salt and pepper.
Add mushroom mixture, bread crumbs and cheese.
Pour into baking dish or oven-proof skillet.
Bake 30 minutes, until set in center and lightly browned.

§ Cheese Soubise §
(Serves 2)

A delicious version of a French country dish.

1/2 onion, sliced
3 slices green bell pepper
2 tablespoons butter or margarine
1 cup cooked rice (leftover or prepared from instant
  package)
1/2 cup chicken broth or bouillon
Dash pepper
2 tablespoons grated cheese

Preheat oven to 325°.
Sauté onion and pepper in butter in skillet until lightly browned.
Stir in rice, pepper and broth.
Spoon into buttered baking dish and cover.
Bake 40 minutes.
Add cheese and stir to melt.

§ Eggs Benedict §
(Serves 1)

This gourmet treat is as easy as stacking a sandwich.

English muffin, toasted
Bacon slice, cooked and crumbled
Egg poached in milk
Hollandaise sauce, canned or homemade (see below)

Place bacon and egg on muffin
Pour sauce over and serve.

§Easy Hollandaise Sauce §

1 egg yolk
1/2 teaspoon lemon juice
Pinch salt
2 tablespoons butter or margarine

Place yolk, lemon juice and salt in blender and blend until smooth,
or use electric mixer.
Melt butter until bubbly.
Slowly pour hot butter into egg and lemon mixture while blending.

§ Easy Quiche §
(Serves 1)

It's easier to prepare than traditional quiche, but it's full of the same rich goodness.

1 slice toast, broken into bite-sized pieces
1 tomato, peeled and sliced
2 slices bacon, cooked and crumbled (optional)
1/2 cup grated cheese (Swiss or cheddar)
1/2 cup milk
1 egg
Pinch salt and pepper
Dash hot pepper sauce
1/4 teaspoon prepared mustard

Preheat oven to 350°.
Place toast pieces in small pie pan or baking dish.
Add tomato slices and bacon.
Sprinkle with grated cheese.
Mix eggs, milk and seasonings and pour over other ingredients.
Bake 30 minutes.

No-Fat Cooking

To avoid using fats in cooking, spray the skillet or baking dish with a non-stick commercial spray when your recipe calls for a greased pan. Another way to avoid fats is by cooking with pans that have been treated with non-stick coating.

§ Egg-in-a-Nest §
(Serves 1)

Margaret Hoffman serves this, along with sliced oranges topped with powdered sugar, to her grandchildren when they come for a visit. "I eat it, too, without the salt," she says. "It's a good breakfast for any age."

    1 tablespoon butter or margarine
    1 slice whole wheat bread
    1 egg
    Dash salt and pepper
    Pinch sweet basil or dill

With knife or cookie cutter, cut hole in bread.
Melt butter in skillet.
Place bread in skillet.
Break egg into hole in bread.
Sauté until light brown and turn.
Continue cooking to taste.
Sprinkle with salt, pepper and herbs.

§ Double Cheese Pudding §
(Serves 1)

Soft, cheesy, rich and tasty.

    1 egg
    1 green onion, chopped
    Dash salt and pepper
    1/4 cup creamed small-curd cottage cheese
    2 tablespoons grated cheddar cheese

Preheat oven to 350°.
Mix all ingredients.
Pour into buttered baking dish.
Bake 20 minutes.

§ Eggs with Corn and Bacon §
(Serves 2)

2 slices bacon
1/2 onion, chopped
1/2 green bell pepper, chopped
1/2 cup creamed corn
Dash salt and pepper
Dash hot pepper sauce
2 eggs, beaten

Fry bacon until crisp, remove from skillet and crumble.
Pour off bacon fat, leaving about 1 tablespoon in skillet.
Sauté onion and green pepper in bacon fat until tender.
Add all other ingredients and cook over medium heat until eggs
   are set.
Sprinkle crumbled bacon over eggs.

Think Zinc

A mineral that is often inadequate in our diet is zinc, which
is essential for many metabolic processes. It helps us resist
disease and infection. Meat, seafood and eggs are good sources
of zinc.

§ Chili Cheese §
(Serves 2)

This is a down-home favorite among those who like a spicy touch of Texas in their chili.

    1 slice bacon
    3 tablespoons chopped onion
    3 tablespoons chopped green or red bell pepper
    1/2 cup cooked kidney beans
    1/3 cup grated cheddar cheese
    1 fresh tomato, chopped, or 1/4 cup tomato sauce
    1/4 teaspoon chili powder or Mixed Hot Spices

Fry bacon until crisp, remove from skillet and crumble.
Sauté onion and pepper in bacon fat.
Add all other ingredients and bacon.
Cook, stirring, 5 minutes.

§ ElRose's Bacon and Eggs §
(Serves 1)

ElRose Groves, hospitable hostess, serves this quick and tasty dish often to her Bed-and-Breakfast guests.

    1 slice bacon, cooked until almost crisp
    1 egg
    2 tablespoons cottage cheese

Preheat oven to 350°.
Line custard cup or other small baking dish with bacon; place in circle around edge of dish.
Break egg into dish.
Spoon cottage cheese over egg.
Place in oven and bake 10 minutes or until egg is done as desired.
Serve with dash of paprika and parsley sprig for color.

§ Egg Foo Yung §
(Serves 2)

1 tablespoon vegetable oil
1/4 cup chopped onion
2 tablespoons chopped celery
1 clove garlic, chopped or pressed
1/2 cup chopped cooked shrimp, pork or chicken
2 tablespoons bean sprouts
3 eggs, lightly beaten
1 teaspoon soy sauce

Sauté onion and celery in oil in skillet until tender but crisp.
Add garlic, shrimp and sprouts and stir.
Mix eggs and soy sauce and pour over.
When eggs are set, fold in half, omelet-style.

§ Bacon and Potato Eggs §
(Serves 2)

1 potato, cooked and sliced
2 slices bacon
2 eggs
1 tablespoon milk
1/4 teaspoon Mixed Herbs
1/4 cup chopped tomatoes

Fry bacon in skillet until crisp.
Add potato slices and fry until lightly browned.
Mix eggs, milk, herbs and tomatoes.
Pour over potatoes and bacon.
Cook over low heat until eggs are set.

§ Yogurt and Egg Dressing §
(About 2/3 cup)

A combination of flavors that adds zest to any crunchy green salad.
It's low in fat and sodium, too.

1/2 cup plain, low-fat yogurt
1 hardcooked egg, chopped
1 teaspoon curry powder
1 green onion, chopped
Dash pepper

Mix all ingredients and chill.

§ Cheese Puffs §
(Serves 1)

2 slices bread
2 slices Swiss cheese
1/2 cup milk
1 egg

Preheat oven to 350°.
Place cheese between bread slices, sandwich-style.
Place in buttered baking dish.
Combine milk and egg and beat lightly.
Pour milk and egg over bread.
Bake 20 minutes, until puffy.

Substitute Ingredients
Substitutes may be used for many ingredients in our recipes.
Instead of egg, use frozen egg substitute; instead of yogurt, sour
cream or sour cream substitute.

BREAD

§ Super-Muffins §
(12-15 muffins)

One bowl, one fork and a muffin tin—that's all you need to make these easy treats. They pack a lot of nutrition and fiber into a small space, and they freeze well.

    1 egg
    1 cup milk
    1/3 cup vegetable oil
    1 cup white flour
    1/2 cup whole wheat flour
    1/2 cup wheat germ
    2 tablespoons bran (wheat or oat)
    1/4 cup brown sugar
    1/4 cup molasses
    1/2 cup raisins
    1/2 cup grated apple
    1 tablespoon baking powder
    1/2 teaspon salt

Preheat oven to 375°.
Mix egg, milk and oil in bowl.
Stir in all other ingredients, using a fork. Mixture will be lumpy.
Spoon batter into muffin tins, greased or lined with cupcake papers.
Fill 2/3 full.
Bake 20 minutes.

Bake Small
Keep a supply of small containers, saucepans and baking pans on hand, to make it easy to cook for one or two. Many dishes can be baked in custard cups, for example, which will also cut the baking time.

§ Bed-and-Breakfast Bran Muffins §

ElRose Groves and her retired minister husband, Everett, serve delightful breakfasts at their charming Bed-and-Breakfast cottage on Puget Island, Washington. One of ElRose's special treats is this bran muffin, easy to make because "the batter keeps for two to three weeks in the refrigerator. So I can serve fresh-baked muffins to our guests every morning."

    1 cup boiling water
    2-1/2 teaspoons baking soda
    1/2 cup shortening or vegetable oil
    1 cup sugar
    2 eggs, beaten
    2 cups buttermilk
    2-1/2 cups flour
    1 teapspoon salt
    2 cups all-bran cereal
    1 cup bran flake cereal
    1 cup chopped dates or raisins

Add soda to boiling water and allow to cool.
Cream shortening with sugar (or mix oil and sugar).
Add eggs and stir in buttermilk.
Add flour and salt alternately with water and soda mixture.
Stir in cereals and dates or raisins.
Cover batter and store in airtight container in refrigerator. May be stored 2-3 weeks.
When ready to bake, preheat oven to 375°.
Spoon batter into greased muffin tins.
Bake 15-20 minutes.

Appetite Pepper-Uppers

Eat your meal in a different spot from your usual dining area. Move to a comfortable chair in the living room or sit near a window for a change.

§ Wheat Sticks §

Chewy and satisfying: a good substitute for bread or crackers.

1 tablespoon honey
1/4 cup vegetable oil
1/2 cup milk
1 cup whole wheat flour
1 cup wheat germ
1/2 teaspoon salt

Preheat oven to 325°.
Blend honey, oil and milk.
Add other ingredients and mix.
Knead lightly on floured board.
Roll dough into strips, 1 inch wide and 3 inches long.
Bake 25 minutes. (For crisp sticks, roll thin and bake 20 minutes.)

§ Cornmeal Biscuits §

Piping hot from the oven, Esther MacLaren's cornmeal biscuits go well with almost any meal. For a touch of the South, serve them with ham and honey.

1-1/4 cups flour
3/4 cup cornmeal
4 teaspoons baking powder
1/2 teaspoon salt
1 tablespoon sugar
4 tablespoons shortening or margarine
3/4 cup milk

Preheat oven to 450°.
Sift dry ingredients.
Blend in shortening or margarine.

Add milk.
Knead dough lightly.
Roll to 1/2-inch thickness and cut with 2-inch cookie
    cutter.
Place on baking sheet and bake 15 minutes.

§ Hazel's Quick Coffee Cake §
(8-inch-square baking pan)

Hazel Jensen first tried this recipe fifty years ago. It's been a breakfast
standby for her family, and an afternoon treat for many visitors,
ever since.

2 cups flour
2 teaspoons baking powder
1/2 teaspoon salt
1/2 cup sugar
1/4 teaspoon mace
1 egg, beaten
1 cup milk
2 tablespoons melted butter

Preheat oven to 425°.
Mix dry ingredients.
Add egg, milk and butter and mix.
Pour into buttered baking dish and sprinkle with topping.
Bake 20 minutes.

Topping

2 tablespoons flour
1/2 teaspoon cinnamon
2 tablespoons brown sugar
1 tablespoon soft butter

Mix all ingredients until crumbly.

§ Pineapple Danish §
(Serves 1)

1 slice whole wheat toast
2 tablespoons cream cheese or small-curd cottage cheese
1 slice canned pineapple or 2 tablespoons crushed
   pineapple
1/2 teaspoon cinnamon
Dash nutmeg

Preheat broiler.
Spread toast with cheese.
Top with pineapple and sprinkle with spices.
Broil until heated, about 3 minutes.

§ Oatcakes §
(6 pancakes)

A hearty, nutty version of the usual breakfast pancake, this one full of nutritious oats.

1/2 cup white flour
1/3 cup uncooked oats
1 tablespoon oat bran (optional)
2 teaspoons baking powder
1/4 teaspoon cinnamon
1/2 cup low-fat or skim milk
1 egg, beaten
1 tablespoon vegetable oil or melted butter

Heat griddle or skillet and oil lightly.
Combine all ingredients, stirring just until mixed.
Spoon batter on hot griddle to size of cake desired. Turn once, when edges are lightly browned.
Serve with jam, syrup, or puréed fruit topping.

Battle Cholesterol With Oat Bran
When you add a spoonful of oats or oat bran to a meat loaf, casserole, batch or cookies, or other food, you may be lowering your risk of cardiovascular disease—the disease which causes more than half of all deaths in the United States. Studies over the past several years show that water-soluble fibers, such as those contained in oats and the more concentrated oat bran, can help to lower blood cholesterol. And that means healthier arteries.

§ Orange-Honey Loaf §
(One 5x9-inch loaf pan)

An orange-flavored, cake-like bread that keeps well. Soaked with a marmalade glaze, it's delicious for breakfast, afternoon tea, or dessert at dinner.

1/2 cup (1 cube) butter or margarine
1/2 cup honey
2 eggs, beaten
3 tablespoons orange marmalade (low-sugar, if possible)
1-1/2 cups white flour
2 tablespoons baking powder
1/4 teaspoon salt
1/4 teaspoon baking soda
1 tablespoon grated orange or lemon peel
1/4 cup chopped nuts

Preheat oven to 325°.
Mix butter and honey.
Add eggs and marmalade and beat well.
Add flour, baking powder, salt and soda, and mix.
Stir in orange or lemon peel and nuts.
Pour into buttered loaf pan (5x9-inch).
Bake 1 hour.
Pierce top with fork at 1-inch intervals, and pour glaze over.

Glaze

2 tablespoons butter or margarine
2 tablespoons orange marmalade
2 tablespoons powdered confectioner's sugar

Melt butter in saucepan.
Stir in marmalade and heat.
Add sugar, stir and heat.

§ Blueberry Sweet Bread §
(One 9x5-inch loaf pan)

With blueberries available year-round, you can make this delicious bread any time. Esther MacLaren, who contributes the recipe, cautions that it's best to use frozen, unthawed berries.

2 cups white flour
1/2 cup sugar
2 teaspoons baking powder
1/2 teaspoon salt
1/2 teaspoon baking soda
2 teaspoons grated orange peel
2 cups *frozen* blueberries
1 egg, lightly beaten
3/4 cup orange juice
2 tablespoons vegetable oil

Topping

3 tablespoons sugar
1 tablespoon cinnamon
2 tablespoons melted butter or margarine

Preheat oven to 350°.
With fork or wooden spoon, mix flour, sugar, salt, soda, baking powder and orange peel.
Fold in blueberries.
Add eggs, orange juice, and oil, stirring carefully.
Pour batter into greased 9x5-inch loaf pan.
Mix topping ingredients and sprinkle on bread batter.
Bake 50-60 minutes or until toothpick inserted in center comes out clean.

§ Best-Yet Walnut Bread §
(One 8x4-inch loaf pan)

Beth Donaldson perfected this recipe. She says, "It's festive enough for teatime, but don't let it fool you. This bread is hearty food and grand for lunchbox sandwiches." It's lower in fat than many sweet breads because it contains no butter or oil.

1 egg
1 cup sugar
3 cups sifted flour
2 tablespoons wheat germ
1 teaspoon salt
4 teaspoons baking powder
1 cup milk
1 cup coarsely chopped walnuts

Preheat oven to 350°.
Combine egg and sugar and beat well.
Mix in all other ingredients except nuts.
Stir in nuts.
Spoon into greased loaf pan and bake 1 hour.

Vitamin and Mineral Supplements: Do you need them?
The best source of advice on dietary supplements is your doctor or dietitian. Your balanced diet may be enough, or your individual needs may call for additional vitamins or minerals. Don't waste your money on unnecessary supplements, and don't endanger your health with megadoses. Get professional advice.

§ Granny's Baking Powder Biscuits §

1 cup flour
2 tablespoons wheat germ
1 tablespoon baking powder
1/2 teaspoon salt
2 tablespoons vegetable oil
5 tablespoons milk

Preheat oven to 400°.
Combine dry ingredients.
Mix oil and milk and stir into flour mixture.
Place between two sheets waxed paper and knead lightly.
Roll out 1/2-inch thick, and cut with biscuit cutter.
Place on baking sheet and bake 12 minutes, until browned.

§ Blueberry Oatmeal Muffins §
(Makes about 12)

Esther MacLaren, always noted for her efficiency, keeps the dry ingredients for this recipe in a quart jar in the cupboard. When she's ready to bake, all she has to do is add the liquids. The result is a flavorful, nutritious muffin that is good any time of day.

1-1/4 cups oats
1 cup whole wheat flour
1 tablespoon baking powder
1/3 cup sugar
1/2 teaspoon salt
1 cup milk
1 egg, lightly beaten
1/4 cup vegetable oil
3/4 cup blueberries, fresh or forzen

Preheat oven to 425°.
Combine dry ingredients.
Add egg, milk, oil and stir just until blended.
Stir in berries.
Spoon into greased muffin tins or tins lined with cupcake papers.
Bake 20-25 minutes.

§ Spicy Baked Pancake §
(Serves 1)

This light pancake puffs to a golden brown as it bakes. Philip Shaw, who contributed the recipe, doubles it to serve two generously when he's making a weekend brunch. Served with an assortment of jams, hot coffee, and a dish of fresh fruit on the side, it makes a toothsome meal that is easy to prepare.

1 egg, lightly beaten
1/4 cup flour
1/4 cup milk
1/8 teaspoon Mixed Sweet Spices
1 tablespoon butter or margarine
1 tablespoon confectioner's powdered sugar
Lemon wedge

Preheat oven to 400°.
Combine egg, milk, flour, and spices and mix to lumpy batter.
Melt butter or margarine in oven-proof skillet.
Pour in batter.
Bake 15 minutes, until pancake is golden brown.
Sprinkle with sugar and lemon juice.

Avoid Spoilage

As our senses dim with age, we run a greater risk of eating foods that have lost their freshness. Watch the dates on milk and yogurt cartons, and don't keep opened foods longer than a few days in the refrigerator. Fresh meat should not be kept longer than one or, at the most, two days before cooking. If in doubt, throw it out. Saving a few cents is not worth the risk to your health.

VEGETABLES & FRUITS

§ Mashed Potatoes Plus §
(Serves 2)

A souffle' -like dish that's full of dairy goodness. With a crisp green vegetable or salad, it makes a meal.

> 1/2 cup hot mashed potatoes (1 cooked potato or 1/3 cup instant packaged potato buds)
> 1/4 cup milk
> 1/4 teaspoon salt
> 1 tablespoon butter, melted
> 1 egg, separated
> 1 tablespoon lemon juice
> 2 tablespoons grated cheddar or Swiss cheese

Preheat oven to 375°.
Mix milk, salt, butter and egg yolks with mashed potatoes.
Beat egg whites until stiff peaks form.
Fold whites into potato mixture.
Stir in lemon juice.
Place in buttered baking dish and top with cheese.
Bake 20 minutes.

Contrast Aids Appetites

When you serve soft foods, such as mashed potatoes and gelatin salad, contrast them with crunchy dishes like cucumbers and broccoli. Contrast colors, too, so your plate will seem appealing. Foods come in so many colors, you can make your plate as colorful as an artist's palette—and that will please your palate.

§ Mildred's Tomato-Cheese Soup §
(Serves 1)

Mildred Waters, an active 90-year-old artist from Laguna Beach, California, often prepares this nutritious soup for a light supper.

    1/2 cup stewed tomatoes
    2 tablespoons Swiss or cheddar cheese, grated
    1 egg

Place tomatoes in saucepan, bring to boil and simmer to reduce
    liquid.
Add cheese.
Beat egg slightly and stir into tomato-cheese mixture.
Serve hot with buttered toast.

§ Ginger Carrots §
(Serves 1)

The gentle bite of ginger and garlic combine with the natural sweetness of vitamin-rich carrots for a taste-pleasing vegetable dish.

    1/2 carrot, cut in slivers
    1 tablespoon butter or margarine
    1/4 teaspoon chopped fresh ginger
    1 clove garlic, chopped or pressed
    1/4 cup white wine or water

Sauté carrot slivers in butter or margarine in skillet.
Add ginger and garlic and stir (do not brown).
Add wine or water, cover and simmer 5-8 minutes.
Remove cover and simmer until liquid evaporates.

§ Potato Nachos §
(Serves 1)

When you're in the mood for a quick, hot snack, try this nutritious version of nachos, the popular cheese-covered chips.

1 potato, cut in 1/4-inch slices (peel if desired)
1/4 cup cheddar cheese

Preheat oven to 375°.
Place potato slices in single layer on buttered baking sheet.
Bake 15 minutes.
Turn potatoes and sprinkle with cheese.
Bake 10 minutes.

§ Onions au Gratin §
(Serves 2)

Rich in flavor and distinctively spicy.

1/2 onion, chopped
2 tablespoons butter or margarine
2 tablespoons flour
Dash salt and pepper
Few drops hot pepper sauce
1/4 teaspoon cumin
1/2 cup grated cheddar cheese

Preheat oven to 350°.
Sauté onions in butter in skillet until tender and remove from heat.
Add all other ingredients, reserving 2 tablespoons cheese.
Place mixture in greased baking dish or custard cups and sprinkle
    with reserved cheese.
Bake uncovered 20 minutes.

§ Pineapple Beets §
(Serves 2)

1/3 canned pineapple chunks, drained
3 tablespoons liquid from drained pineapple
1 tablespoon vinegar
1/2 teaspoon cornstarch
1/4 teaspoon Mixed Sweet Spices
1 cup (1 small can) sliced beets, drained

Place all ingredients except pineapple chunks and beets in saucepan
and mix well.
Simmer, stirring, until thickened.
Add beets and pineapple and heat.

§ Vegetable-Rice §
(Serves 2)

1/4 cup uncooked rice, brown or white
1 tablespoon vegetable oil
1/2 potato, diced (peel if preferred)
1/2 carrot, diced (peel if preferred)
1/3 cup fresh chopped green beans (or 4 tablespoons
frozen)
1/2 teaspoon Mixed Hot Spices
1 clove garlic, minced or pressed
1/8 teaspoon minced fresh ginger
1 cup chicken broth or bouillon

Heat oil in saucepan.
Add potato, carrot and beans and sauté, stirring, 1 minute.
Add all other ingredients except broth and cook 2 minutes.
Add broth and bring to boil.
Cover and simmer 20 minutes for white rice, 45 minutes for brown
rice.

§ Quick-Stuffed Baked Potato §
(Serves 1)

1 medium potato, washed, unpeeled
1/4 cup cooked chili, with or without meat
3 tablespoons grated cheddar cheese

Preheat oven to 400°.
Bake potato 50 minutes.
Heat chili in saucepan.
Split potato; pour chili over.
Top with cheese.
Place potato on aluminum foil under broiler; broil until cheese melts.

§ Potatoes and Green Beans §
(Serves 1)

1/2 potato, sliced
1/4 cup fresh green beans, chopped
1 teaspoon butter or margarine
1/2 teaspoon dill
Dash salt
1 tablespoon grated cheddar cheese

Place potato slices in saucepan.
Place beans on potatoes.
Add water to cover (about 1/3 cup).
Cover, bring to boil and simmer 10 minutes.
Drain and add all other ingredients.
Cover and remove from heat.
Serve when cheese has melted.

§ French Onion Soup §
(Serves 1)

4 tablespoons dried onion soup mix
1/4 onion, sliced
1 tablespoon vegetable oil
Thick slice French bread
2 tablespoons grated Parmesan cheese

Prepare soup according to package directions, using 1 cup water.
Sauté onion slices in oil in skillet.
Add soup to skillet and simmer.
Place French bread in soup bowl and ladle soup over it.
Sprinkle with cheese.
Place under broiler a few seconds to melt cheese.

§ Summer Soup §
(Serves 2)

A chilled vegetable soup, perfect for a hot summer evening.

1 cup chopped broccoli
2 cups chicken broth or bouillon
1/2 onion, chopped
1 tablespoon butter or margarine or vegetable oil
1/4 teaspoon salt
Dash pepper
Dash nutmeg
1/4 teaspoon curry powder
1 teaspoon chopped parsley
1 tablespoon lemon juice

Sauté onion in butter or oil in skillet until tender.
Add all other ingredients except lemon juice.
Simmer 10 minutes.
Cool, then purée in blender or food processor.
Add lemon juice and chill in refrigerator 4 hours or more.

§ Creamy Tomato Soup §
(Serves 2)

A low-sodium special that costs little and is simple to prepare and home-made delicious.

    1 tablespoon butter or margarine (unsalted if possible)
    1 tablespoon flour
    Dash pepper
    1/4 teaspoon dill
    1/4 teaspoon marjoram
    1 cup milk
    1/2 cup tomato sauce
    Few drops hot pepper sauce

Melt butter in saucepan.
Add flour and pepper, stirring until flour bubbles.
Add milk and cook until thick, stirring constantly.
Add all other ingredients and stir until smooth. Heat but do not
  boil.

Emergency Planning
Be prepared for bad weather or days when you're unable to get to the grocery store. Stock an emergency shelf with nonfat instant powdered milk, peanut butter, canned soups and fruits, canned fish and stews. If you have a freezer, keep a week's supply of meat, bread and vegetables on hand. Cheese and milk may also be frozen.

§ Potato-Onion Soup §
(Serves 2)

Easy and quick to make with dried, packaged potatoes.

    1/2 cup water
    1/2 onion, chopped
    1 chicken bouillon cube
    1 cup low-fat or skim milk
    1/2 cup instant packaged mashed potatoes
    Chopped parsley

Combine water, onion and bouillon in saucepan and heat to
  boiling.
Stir in milk and instant potatoes and heat. Thin with more milk,
if desired.
Sprinkle with parsley and serve.

§ Pineapple-Carrots §
(Serves 1)

    1/2 carrot, minced
    2 tablespoons crushed pineapple, drained
    1 teaspoon butter or margarine
    Dash salt
    1 tablespoon rum (optional)
    1/4 teaspoon Mixed Sweet Spices

Preheat oven to 350°.
Steam carrots in saucepan with 1/4 cup water 10 minutes.
Place carrots and all other ingredients in buttered baking dish.
Bake 10 minutes.

§ Green Beans Parmesan §
(Serves 2)

Parmesan cheese dresses up an ordinary green vegetable and turns it into a party fare.

> 1 tablespoon chopped onion
> 1 tablespoon butter or margarine
> 1/2 cup green beans, fresh or frozen
> 3 tablespoons water
> Pinch salt
> 1/4 teaspoon sweet basil, fresh or dried
> 3 tablespoons grated Parmesan cheese

Sauté onion in butter in saucepan until lightly browned.
Add all other ingredients except cheese.
Cover and simmer until tender, about 12 minutes.
Sprinkle with cheese.

§ Garden Stew §
(Serves 2, with leftovers)

This meal-in-a-dish is a favorite of Eudora Benson, a retired book-keeper who loves to eat but is much too busy planning her next travel adventure to spend much time in the kitchen. "Just remember, it's a quarter cup of everything," she says.

> 1/4 cup *each*:
> chopped broccoli, fresh or frozen
> grated cheddar cheese
> chopped mushrooms, fresh or canned
> evaporated milk
> bacon, fried crisp and crumbled (2 slices)
> chopped onion

Preheat oven to 350°.
Place broccoli in buttered baking dish.
Cover with cheese.
Add bacon and mushrooms.
Pour milk over all.
Bake uncovered 20 minutes.
Remove from oven, place onions on top, and bake 10 minutes more.

§ Fried Rice §
(Serves 2)

1 tablespoon vegetable oil
1 tablespoon chopped onion
1 tablespoon chopped green bell pepper
1/2 cup cooked rice, white or brown
2 tablespoons chopped, canned water chestnuts (optional)
3 mushrooms, sliced
2 teaspoons soy sauce
1 egg, lightly beaten

Sauté onion, green pepper and mushrooms in vegetable oil until
  tender but crisp.
Add rice, water chestnuts and soy sauce.
Cook 5 minutes, stirring often.
Add egg.
Cook 3 minutes, stirring constantly.

Appetite Pepper-Uppers

—Pay attention to how food looks, just as you do with guests.
A parsley garnish or a curl of orange peel add to the attractive
appearance of your meal. It will taste better if it looks good
to eat.

§ Carolyn's Ratatouille §
(Serves 8)

Our consulting dietitian makes a big batch of this tasty vegetable stew and freezes part of it. After a busy day, all she has to do is heat it for a nutritious supper. It has only 50 calories per cup.

1 eggplant, peeled and cut in 1/2-inch cubes
6 medium zucchini, peeled and sliced thickly
2 green or red bell peppers, seeded and cut in chunks
2 stalks celery, cut in diagonal slices
2 cloves garlic, minced
2-3 tablespoons chopped parsley
1/4 teaspoon pepper
1 teaspoon oregano
2 tablespoon vinegar
Dash hot pepper sauce
6 cups diced, canned tomatoes
2 cups chopped fresh mushrooms

In soup kettle, combine all ingredients except mushrooms.
Cover, bring to a boil, and simmer over low heat 20 minutes.
Remove cover and cook over moderate heat 15 more minutes,
 stirring to prevent scorching.
Add mushrooms, heat, and serve.

More Flavor, Not Less
Contrary to popular belief, older people do not usually need bland diets with fewer seasonings. The opposite is true; as our tastebuds become less sensitive with age, we need more flavor-enhancing, not less. Experiment with herbs and spices to find combinations that lend zest to the foods you eat.

§ Spanish Rice §
(Serves 1)

1 tablespoon vegetable oil
2 tablespoons chopped green bell pepper
2 tablespoons chopped onion
1 clove garlic, minced
1/4 teaspoon sweet basil
1/4 cup uncooked white or brown rice
1/4 cup chopped tomato, fresh or canned
1/8 teaspoon salt
1/8 teaspoon oregano
Dash pepper
1/2 cup water

Sauté green pepper and onion in oil in skillet until tender.
Add garlic and basil and stir.
Add all other ingredients and cover.
Simmer 20 minutes for white rice and 45 minutes for brown rice.

§ Corn Chowder §
(Serves 2, with leftovers)

Creamy and delicious with old-fashioned corn flavor.

2 tablespoons vegetable oil
1 tablespoon chopped onion
1 celery stalk
2 tablespoons flour
Dash pepper
1 chicken bouillon cube
1/4 cup water
1 cup milk
1 medium cooked potato, chopped

1 small can creamed corn
Chopped parsley

Sauté onion and celery in oil in saucepan.
Stir in flour and pepper and heat until bubbly.
Dissolve bouillon cube in water and stir into flour mixture.
Add milk and stir until thickened.
Add potato and creamed corn and simmer 2-3 minutes. Do not boil.
If chowder is too thick, add milk to thin.
Sprinkle each serving with parsley.

§ Lentils and Rice §

1/4 cup chopped onion
1/2 cup cooked brown rice
1/2 cup cooked lentils
1 egg, slightly beaten
1/4 teaspoon salt
1 clove garlic, minced
1/2 cup dry bread cubes
1/2 cup canned tomatoes
1/2 teaspoon Mixed Hot Spices

Preheat oven to 350°.
Mix all ingredients and pour into oiled baking dish.
Bake 30 minutes. Serve with catsup or heated, canned cream soup.

Chewing Solutions

Prepare soups, stews or casserole dishes instead of chops and steaks.

§ Lentil Soup §
(Serves 2 generously)

A soup with hearty, robust goodness—perfect for a cold winter's night.

    1/2 cup uncooked lentils
    4 cups water
    1 pork or ham bone
    1/4 cup chopped celery
    1/4 cup chopped carrots
    2 tablespoons chopped onion
    Dash pepper

Place all ingredients in large saucepan.
Bring to boil, turn down heat and simmer about 2 hours.
Remove ham or pork bone, cut any meat from bone and place in soup.
Season to taste.

§ Carrot-Raisin Salad §
(Serves 1)

    1 small carrot, grated
    1/4 cup raisins
    1/4 teaspoon fresh ginger, chopped
    1 teaspoon plain, low-fat yogurt
    Dash nutmeg
    Lettuce

To plump raisins, cover with water in saucepan and bring to boil.
Remove from heat and set aside 5 minutes, then drain.
Mix all ingredients and chill.
Serve on bed of chopped lettuce.

§ Apple-Carrot Slaw §
·(Serves 2)

1/2 cup shredded cabbage
2 tablespoons grated carrots
1/4 cup nuts, chopped
1/2 apple, chopped
2 tablespoons raisins

Dressing

2 tablespoons yogurt
1/4 cup cottage cheese
2 tablespoons apple juice

Mix all ingredients except dressing.
Place Dressing ingredients in blender or food processor and mix
  until smooth.
Pour Dressing over mixed salad.

§ Waldorf Delight §
(Serves 1)

1/2 medium apple, chopped
1 teaspoon lemon juice
1 celery stalk, chopped
2 tablespoons mayonnaise
1 tablespoon yogurt
1 teaspoon honey
Lettuce

Sprinkle apple slices with lemon juice and drizzle with honey.
Add all other ingredients and mix well.
Serve on bed of chopped lettuce.

§ Chilled Bean Salad §
(Serves 2)

1/2 cup canned green beans
1/4 red onion, sliced thin
1/4 cup sliced mushrooms, fresh or canned
2 tablespoons vegetable oil
2 tablespoons vinegar

Dressing

2 tablespoons plain yogurt
1 tablespoon mayonnaise
1 clove garlic, pressed or minced
1/4 teaspoon dill weed
1/4 teaspoon lemon juice
1/8 teaspoon dry mustard

Mix all ingredients except Dressing.
Cover and marinate overnight.
Mix Dressing ingredients and chill.
Drain marinated salad, pour Dressing over and serve on lettuce.

Vitamin A: Good and Bad

Vitamin A is necessary to good health—but don't overdo it.
An excess of vitamin A can cause headaches, nausea, diarrhea
and even liver and bone damage. Ask your doctor or dietitian about vitamin A supplements. Daily servings of yellow
and leafy green vegetables may supply all the vitamin A your
body needs.

§ Golden Salad §
(Serves 1)

1/2 carrot, grated
1/2 orange, cut in sections
1/2 teaspoon grated orange rind
Chopped lettuce

Dressing

1 teaspoon honey
2 teaspoons vinegar
1/2 teaspoon soy sauce
2 teaspoons vegetable oil

Place carrot, orange and rind on lettuce.
Mix dressing ingredients and pour over.

§ Coleslaw with Pineapple and Carrots §
(Serves 2)

1/2 cup grated cabbage
1/4 cup grated carrot
1/4 cup canned crushed pineapple or chunk pineapple
1 tablespoon mayonnaise
1 teaspoon lemon juice
1 tablespoon liquid from canned pineapple

Mix all ingredients.
Chill and serve.

§ Classic Macaroni Salad §
(Serves 2 generously)

From Vera Porter's recipe file come this old favorite, a salad both smooth and crunchy, ideal for a summer supper.

1/3 cup mayonnaise
1 tablespoon vinegar
2 teaspoons prepared mustard
1/2 teaspoon sugar
1/2 teaspoon salt
1/8 teaspoon pepper
4 ounces elbow macaroni, cooked and drained
1/2 cup chopped celery
1/2 cup chopped green or red bell pepper
2 tablespoons chopped onion

Mix together mayonnaise, vinegar, and seasonings.
Add remaining ingredients and toss to coat well.
Cover and chill.

Freeze Chopped Onion
To avoid tedious chopping every time you need a tablespoon of chopped onion, cut up several at a time (a food processor is a big help with this) and place them in a container in the freezer. Or freeze small quantities in plastic bags so you'll have just the right amount for your recipes quickly available.

§ Grated Carrot Salad §
(Serves 1)

1/2 carrot, grated
1/4 cup grated zucchini
2 tablespoons walnuts or cashews (optional)
1 teaspoon honey
2 teaspoons vinegar
1/2 teaspoon soy sauce
2 teaspoons vegetable oil

Combine all ingredients and mix well.

§ Minty Fruit Salad §
(Serves 1)

Banana, orange, grapefruit, pear, melon, or other fruits (fresh, frozen or canned)

3 or 4 mint leaves, fresh or dried
1 tablespoon lemon juice
2 tablespoons plain yogurt

Chop fruit to equal 1 cup.
Mix fruit with mint and lemon juice.
Allow to stand 15 minutes.
Top with yogurt and garnish with mint leaf.

---

4 Food Groups
Every day eat at least one item from each of the 4 main food groups: (1) Milk and milk products; (2) Breads and cereals; (3) Vegetables and fruits; (4) Meat, fish, eggs and beans.

§ Baked Apple §
(Serves 1)

1 apple
1 tablespoon brown sugar
1 teaspoon butter or margarine
1/4 teaspoon cinnamon
1 teaspoon raisins

Preheat oven to 400°.
Core apple. (Or cut in half and scoop out core from each half.)
Place apple in baking dish and fill with sugar, butter, cinnamon
  and raisins.
Cover bottom of pan with water (1/4-inch deep).
Bake 30 minutes or until tender when pierced with fork.

§ Cranberry Pears §
(Serves 1)

1 fresh whole pear
1/4 cup cranberry sauce
1 tablespoon lemon juice
Dash allspice

Preheat oven to 350°.
Stand pear in baking dish.
Mix lemon, cranberry sauce and allspice and spoon over pear.
Bake 30 minutes.

Chewing Solutions
Avoid sweets, berries, nuts and other foods that stick easily
in teeth. When nuts are called for in the recipes in this book,
they are almost always optional.

§ Peachy Banana Shake §
(Serves 1)

1/2 cup chopped fresh peach (or 1 jar chopped or puréed
  baby food peaches)
1/2 cup milk, whole or skim
1/2 banana
2 tablespoons lemon juice
1/2 teaspoon minced lemon rind
Dash cloves

Mix all ingredients in blender or food processor until smooth.
Serve as drink or freeze as dessert.

§ Frozen Banana §
(Serves 1)

A treat any time of day. Freezing creates a special texture and brings
out the natural sweetness of the fruit.

1 ripe banana
Plastic wrap

Peel banana and cut in fourths.
Wrap in plastic and place in freezer.

Chewing Solutions
—Have your teeth and gums checked regularly by your den-
tist. If you have dentures, they may need to be replaced. Our
gums and facial muscles change as we age, and dentures may
not fit as well.

DESSERTS

§ Betty's Lemon Cake Pudding §
(Serves 3)

Betty Parkhurst says this tangy dessert has been a favorite with her family in Illinois for 40 years.

1/2 cup sugar
3 tablespoons flour
Dash salt
1 egg, separated
1/2 cup milk
2-1/2 tablespoons lemon juice
1 teaspoon grated lemon rind

Preheat oven to 350°.
Beat egg white until stiff peaks form.
In another bowl, mix sugar, salt, flour and lemon rind.
Add yolk and milk and mix well.
Fold in egg whites. Mixture will be lumpy.
Pour into buttered baking dish.
Set in pan of hot water and bake 50-60 minutes.

Convenience Foods?

Everytime we go to the supermarket, we see new products on the shelves, many of them "instant" packaged foods. Some offer a great saving in time and effort and are well worth the extra expense. Others are not only expensive, they may be high in sodium, fat and preservatives. Protect yourself by using fresh foods where possible, with the occasional addition of a favorite package.

§ Pineapple Betty §
(Serves 2)

Bread pudding texture, with a dash of fruity, spicy pineapple.
Delicious when served warm with milk or ice cream.

    1 slice stale bread
    1/2 cup crushed pineapple
    1 tablespoon brown sugar
    2 teaspoons butter or margarine
    1/2 teaspoon Mixed Sweet Spices

Preheat oven to 350°.
Cut bread into cubes and sprinkle in buttered baking dish.
Cover with pineapple and sugar.
Dot with butter and sprinkle with spices.
Bake 30 minutes.

§ Blueberry Flummery §
(Serves 2)

    1 tablespoon cornstarch
    1/4 cup sugar
    3/4 cup water
    1 cup blueberries, fresh or frozen
    Juice and grated rind of 1 lemon
    1/4 teaspoon Mixed Sweet Spices

Mix cornstarch and sugar in saucepan.
Add all other ingredients.
Cook, stirring, until slightly thickened.
Chill and serve alone or as a sauce on coffee cake, Vyra's Prune Cake
    (page 142) or Orange-Honey Loaf (page 101).

§ Caramel Custard §
(Serves 2)

2 tablespoons brown sugar
1 egg
1/2 cup evaporated milk (skim or regular)
1/3 cup water
2 tablespoons sugar
1 teaspoon vanilla
1 tablespoon rum (optional)

Preheat oven to 350°.
Press 1 spoonful of brown sugar into each of 2 custard cups.
Beat egg.
Add all other ingredients and mix until smooth.
Pour slowly into custard cups, over brown sugar.
Set cups in shallow baking pan and pour hot water in pan, around
    cups (about 1 inch water).
Bake 45 minutes.
Cool, loosen edges with knife, and unmold onto serving dishes.

Dishpan Hands?
Many of our recipes call for very few utensils and pans. To make
clean-up even easier, line your baking pan with aluminum foil.
For some firm-textured dishes, such as meat loaf and bar
cookies, simply fold heavy-duty aluminum foil to create edges,
and you have an instant, disposable pan.

§ Apple-Cran Crisp §
(Serves 3)

2 cups cooking apples, peeled and sliced
1 tablespoon lemon juice
3 tablespoons cranberry sauce, fresh or canned
3 tablespoons flour
3 tablespoons oats
1/4 cup brown sugar
1/4 cup butter or margarine
1 teaspoon Mixed Sweet Spices

Preheat oven to 375°.
Place apples and cranberry sauce in buttered baking dish.
Sprinkle with lemon juice.
Mix all other ingredients with fork or fingers and spoon over
 apple mixture.
Bake 30 minutes. Serve warm, plain or with milk or cream.

§ Apple Spice Cake §
(One 8-inch-square pan)

1/4 cup flour
1-1/2 teaspoons baking soda
1/2 teaspoon salt
1 teaspoon Mixed Sweet Spices
1 tablespoon cocoa
1/2 cup sugar
1/3 cup vegetable oil
1 cup unsweetened applesauce
1/4 cup raisins
1/4 cup chopped nuts (optional)

Preheat oven to 375°.
Mix flour, soda, salt, sugar, spices and cocoa.
In another bowl, combine oil and applesauce.
Add flour mixture and beat until smooth.
Stir in nuts and raisins.
Pour batter into greased 8-inch-square baking pan.
Bake 40 minutes.
Serve topped with applesauce.

§ Dessert Topping §
(Serves 2)

2 tablespoons ice water
2 tablespoons instant non-fat powdered milk
2 tablespoons sugar
2 tablespoon lemon juice

Slowly add powdered milk to ice water, beating until stiff peaks form
(about 10 minutes).
Add sugar and lemon juice.
Chill.

§ Macaroon Torte §
(One 8-inch-square pan)

Esther McLeod contributes this sweet and chewy, easy-to-make treat.

2 egg whites
1/4 cup sugar
1/2 teaspoon baking powder
7 saltines (soda crackers), rolled to make fine crumbs
1/4 cup chopped dates
1/4 cup chopped nuts

Preheat oven to 300°.

Beat egg whites until foamy.

Slowly add sugar and baking powder, continuing to beat until soft peaks form.

Fold in cracker crumbs, dates and nuts.

Spoon into buttered 8-inch square baking pan.

Bake 40 minutes. Serve plain or with ice cream or whipped topping, sprinkled with chopped dates or nuts.

§ Aunt Esther's Wacky Cake §
(One 8-inch square pan)

A chocolatey-good dessert in great demand for 3 generations of Esther MacLaren's family reunions. Esther comments: "When I first tried this recipe, I didn't believe it would work. But it does!"

1-1/2 cups white flour
1 cup sugar
1 teaspoon baking soda
3 tablespoons baking cocoa
1 teaspoon salt
1 teaspoon vanilla
1 tablespoon vinegar
5 tablespoons vegetable oil
1 cup cold water
1/2 cup chopped nuts (optional)

Preheat oven to 325°.

Sift flour, sugar, baking soda, cocoa and salt directly into 8-inch square baking pan.

Make 3 hollows in mixture.

In one dent, pour vanilla. In another dent, pour vinegar. In the third dent, pour oil.

Pour water over all and stir until smooth.
If nuts are used, sprinkle over batter.
Bake 25 minutes.

§ Pudding Mix §

Make your own mix of dry ingredients and keep it on hand for almost-instant dessert preparation.

2/3 cup powdered milk
3 tablespoons cornstarch
1/3 cup sugar
2 cups water
Dash salt
Vanilla Pudding: 1 tablespoon vanilla flavoring
Chocolate Pudding: 1/4 cup baking cocoa
Caramel Pudding: 1/4 cup brown sugar instead of white

Mix all ingredients in saucepan and heat, stirring until thickened. Chill and serve.

Vitamin D
A well-balanced diet and regular outdoor activity give most of us the vitamin D we require; high dosage supplements can be dangerous, for they may lead to kidney damage. Consult your doctor or dietitian before taking extra vitamin D.

§ Prune Whip §
(Serves 2)

1/2 cup cooked, drained, chopped prunes
2 egg whites
2 tablespoons sugar
Dash salt
1 teaspoon lemon juice
1/4 teaspoon chopped lemon rind
1/2 teaspoon cinnamon

Beat egg whites until foamy.
Add prunes, sugar, salt and cinnamon and beat until stiff peaks
  form.
Add lemon juice and rind.
Spoon into parfait or sherbet glasses and chill.

§ Oat Wheat Cookies §

1/2 cup shortening
1/4 cup butter or margarine
1/4 cup white sugar
3/4 cup brown sugar
2 eggs
1 teaspoon vanilla
1 teaspoon lemon rind, grated or minced
2 tablespoons molasses
1-1/2 cups white flour
2 tablespoons wheat germ
2 tablespoons oat bran
2 cups oats
1 teaspoon baking soda
1/2 teaspoon salt
1/2 teaspoon Mixed Sweet Spices

Preheat oven to 375°.
Mix shortening, butter and sugar and beat until creamy.
Add eggs, vanilla, and lemon rind.
Add all other ingredients and mix well.
Place walnut-sized pieces of dough on baking sheet.
Bake 12 minutes. (1 cup raisins, coconut, nuts or dates may be added
   to dough, if desired.)

§ Bernice's Oatmeal Cookies §
(About 75 small cookies)

Bernice Peck knows the value of oats to good health; she also knows the importance of good taste. This cookie recipe is one of her favorites.

   1 cup shortening
   3/4 cup sugar
   2 eggs
   2 cups oatmeal
   1 cup flour
    1/2 teaspoon baking soda
   1/3 cup milk (skim, low-fat, or whole)
   1 teaspoon cinnamon
   1 teaspoon vanilla
   1/2 teaspoon salt
   1/2 cup raisins, chopped nuts, or chopped dates (optional)

Preheat oven to 350°.
Beat shortening, sugar and eggs until creamy.
Mix in all other ingredients except nuts, raisins or dates.
Stir in nuts, raisins or dates.
Place spoonfuls of dough on baking sheet.
Bake 8-10 minutes.

§ Lemon or Orange Sherbet §
(Serves 2 generously)

A low-sodium, low-fat treat that tastes as good as the best iced desserts.

    1 egg, separated
    3 tablespoons sugar
    3 tablespoons lemon or orange juice
    1/2 teaspoon lemon or orange rind, grated or minced
    3 tablespoons water
    3 tablespoons instant non-fat powdered milk

Add water and powdered milk to egg white and beat until
    mixture forms stiff peaks.
In another bowl, combine egg yolk, sugar, lemon or
    orange juice and rind.
Fold yolk mixture into egg white mixture.
Spoon into shallow pan (or ice cube tray) and freeze.

§ Vyra's Prune Cake §
(One 8-inch-square pan)

A fruit-filled goodie that Vyra Hamilton often serves with tea and coffee to afternoon visitors.

    1/2 cup sugar
    2 tablespoons butter or margarine
    2 eggs
    1/2 cup cooked, chopped prunes
    1 teaspoon baking soda dissolved in 1 tablespoon prune
        juice
    1 cup white or whole wheat flour
    1 teaspoon Mixed Sweet Spices
    1 teaspoon baking powder

Preheat oven to 350°.
Beat sugar, butter and eggs until creamy.
Add prunes and juice with baking soda.
Add flour, spices and baking powder.
Spoon into greased 8-inch-square baking pan.
Bake 30 minutes.

§ Coconut Squares §
(One 8-inch-square pan)

1-1/4 cups white flour
1/2 cup (1 cube) butter or margarine
2 teaspoons brown sugar

Preheat oven to 350°.
Mix ingredients and press into baking pan.
Pour filling over.

Filling

3/4 cup brown sugar
2 eggs, lightly beaten
1 cup flaked coconut
1/2 cup chopped walnuts
1 teaspoon vanilla

Mix all ingredients and pour over first mixture in baking pan.
Bake 35 minutes.

§ Peanut Butter Squares §
(One 8-inch-square pan)

Chewy desserts with peanut protein, perfected by Hilda Janowski, 78 years young and still a peanut butter lover.

1/3 cup peanut butter, creamy or chunky style
1/3 cup butter or margarine
1/2 teaspoon vanilla
3/4 cup brown sugar
1/4 teaspoon salt
1 egg (or 1/4 cup frozen egg substitute)
2/3 cup white flour
1 tablespoon wheat germ
1/4 cup chopped peanuts (optional)

Preheat oven to 350°.
Mix peanut butter and butter.
Add vanilla, sugar, salt and egg and blend well.
Add flour and wheat germ and beat until smooth.
Stir in nuts.
Spread in buttered baking pan.
Bake 30 minutes.

§ Prune-Apple Bars §
(One 8-inch-square baking pan)

Natural sweetness sandwiched between nutritious grains.

1/2 cup brown sugar
2/3 cup white flour
1/2 teaspoon salt
1/4 teaspoon baking soda
1 cup rolled oats, regular or quick-cooking
2 tablespoons oat bran

1 teaspoon Mixed Sweet Spices
6 tablespoons butter or margarine, melted
1 cup applesauce, fresh or canned
1/2 cup cooked chopped prunes

Preheat oven to 375°.
Combine all dry ingredients.
Add melted butter and mix.
Spoon half of mixture into greased 8-inch-square baking pan and
   press with hand or spatula.
Mix applesauce and chopped prunes and spread over flour mixture.
Top with remaining flour mixture.
Bake 20 minutes, until golden brown.

§ Frozen Strawberry Pie §
(One 10-inch pie)

Vera Porter shares two of her favorite strawberry pie recipes. This
one calls for frozen berries, the next for fresh—each is delicious.

2 egg whites
1 teaspoon lemon juice
2/3 cup sugar (or 1/4 cup if berries are sweetened)
Dash salt
2 cups frozen strawberries, thawed
1/2 cup whipping cream
1 teaspoon vanilla
1 baked pie shell

Beat egg white until foamy.
Add lemon juice, sugar and salt and beat until stiff peaks form.
Whip cream and add vanilla.
Fold cream into strawberry mixture.

Spoon into pie shell. (Or spoon into dessert dishes and serve as
  pudding.)
Chill or freeze.
Serve garnished with strawberries and fresh mint leaves, if available.

§ Vera's Fresh Strawberry Pie §
(One 9-inch pie)

1 baked pie shell
1 cup fresh strawberries
2 cups vanilla pudding (packaged, or see recipe, page 139)
Whipped topping (page 137)

Stir berries into prepared pudding.
Spoon into pie shell (or serving dishes), top with whipped
  topping and chill.

§ Star Cookies §

Another of Vera Porter's specialties, these rich cookies are easy to
make and festive for holidays.

1 cup butter or margarine
2 cups white flour
1/2 cup sugar
1/2 cup finely chopped nuts
Chocolate candy "stars"

Mix all ingredients except chocolate.
Chill dough several hours or overnight.
Preheat oven to 350°.
Shape dough into walnut-sized balls and place on baking sheet.

Bake 10 minutes.
Remove from oven and press a chocolate star firmly into each cookie.
Return to oven for 5 minutes.

§ Cherry Crumb Crunch §
(One 8-inch-square pan)

Esther MacLaren's afternoon and after-dinner visitors give this unusual dessert a top rating. It gets compliments every time it is served.

  1/4 cup butter or margarine
  3/4 cup white flour
  1/2 cup brown sugar
  1/2 cup oats
  1/2 cup chopped nuts (optional)
  1/4 teaspoon baking soda
  1/4 teaspoon salt
  1/4 teaspoon cloves
  1 can (16-ounce) pitted pie cherries, drained

Preheat oven to 350°.
Combine all ingredients except cherries. Mix with fingers until
  crumbly.
Spread 1/2 mixture in 8-inch-square pan.
Spoon cherries over.
Top with remaining crumb mixture.
Bake 30-35 minutes.

Food Storage
Use your refrigerator to store items often kept in the cupboard. Raisins, nuts, bread, coffee, jams and jellies, shortening and peanut butter will all keep longer if chilled.

§ Chocolate Applesauce Cake §
(One 8-inch-square pan)

Edith Owenbey says this recipe came from a pioneer family in Utah. Moist and spicy, the cake is as popular as ever. It keeps well, refrigerated.

1/2 cup sugar
1 cup white flour
1/2 teaspoon cinnamon
1/2 teaspoon nutmeg
1/2 teaspoon cloves
1-1/2 teaspoons cornstarch
2 tablespoons unsweetened cocoa
1/2 cup melted butter or margarine or vegetable oil
3/4 cup unsweetened applesauce
1 teaspoon baking soda

Preheat oven to 350°.
Mix sugar, flour, spices, cornstarch and cocoa.
Stir in butter or oil.
Add baking soda to applesauce and mix with batter.
Pour into 8-inch-square baking pan.
Bake 1 hour. (1 cup nuts, raisins or candied fruit may be added before baking, if desired).

§ Edith's Oatmeal Cookies §

Another of Edith Owenbey's contributions, these delectable morsels will help add all-important oats to your diet.

1/2 cup white sugar
1/2 cup brown sugar
1/2 cup shortening
1 egg

1 cup oats
1 cup flour
1/2 teaspoon baking soda dissolved in 1 teaspoon hot
    water
1/2 teaspoon salt
1/2 teaspoon vanilla

Preheat oven to 350°.
Beat sugar, shortening and eggs until smooth.
Add all other ingredients and mix.
Place by spoonfuls on baking sheet and bake 12-15 minutes.
(Add 1/2 cup chopped nuts or raisins to dough before baking, if
    desired).

§ Cinnamon Apple Pudding §
(Serves 2 generously)

Not too sweet, not too tart—a dessert or breakfast treat that goes
well with milk or ice cream.

2 cooking apples, peeled and sliced
1 tablespoon lemon juice
2 teaspoons sugar or honey
1/2 teaspoon cinnamon
1 egg
2 teaspoons brown sugar
1 tablespoon butter or margarine
1/4 cup flour
1/4 teaspoon baking powder

Preheat oven to 350°.
Place apples in baking pan.
Sprinkle with lemon juice, sugar or honey and cinnamon.

Beat egg, sugar and butter in mixing bowl.
Add flour and baking powder to egg mixture.
Spread batter over apples.
Bake 30 minutes, until golden brown and apples are tender.

§ Grape Yogurt Fluff §
(Serves 2)

1/2 cup plain yogurt
1 tablespoon lemon juice
3 tablespoons grape juice (other fruit juice may be
   substituted)
1 teaspoon grated lemon rind
2 teaspoons sugar
1-1/2 teaspoon (1/2 envelope) unflavored gelatin
3 tablespoons cold water
1 egg white

Mix yogurt, lemon juice, grape juice, lemon rind and sugar.
Mix gelatin with cold water in small saucepan and heat to dissolve.
Add gelatin and water to yogurt.
Refrigerate until thickened.
Beat egg white until stiff peaks form.
Fold egg white into yogurt mixture and chill.

Shop Without Anxiety
Instead of clinging to a pocketbook to protect your shopping
money and coupons, wear a small purse, attached to a ribbon,
around your neck. It can be tucked inside a jacket or sweater
and pulled out when you're at the cashier's counter.

§ Frozen Fruity Yogurt §
(1 serving)

1/2 cup plain yogurt
1/2 cup chopped fresh or canned, drained fruit
1/4 teaspoon vanilla
1 teaspoon sugar or honey

Mix all ingredients and freeze until slushy.
Stir and refreeze.
Allow to thaw slightly before serving.

§ Sweet Potato Pudding §
(Serves 2 generously)

1 egg
3/4 cup evaporated milk
3/4 cup cooked, mashed sweet potatoes (yams)
1/4 cup brown sugar
Dash salt
1 teaspoon Mixed Sweet Spices

Preheat oven to 350°.
Combine all ingredients and pour mixture into baking dish.
Bake 40 minutes.

On A Budget
If you're a shopper on a budget (and who isn't?), choose wisely. Buy sale items in quantity and divide your purchases into smaller packages for the freezer (be sure to label them clearly). Try splitting costs and purchases with a friend or relative.

§ Yogurt Banana Split §
(Serves 1)

1/2 cup plain yogurt
3 tablespoons fresh or frozen strawberries
1/2 banana
Chopped nuts
Honey or heated strawberry jam
Dessert Topping (optional—see page 137)
Chopped nuts

Spoon yogurt into parfait glass or dessert bowl.
Spoon strawberries over yogurt.
Slice bananas lengthwise and place on either side of yogurt.
Drizzle honey or jam over all.
Top with whipped topping and nuts.

§ Hawaiian Ice §
(Serves 2)

Fluffy and light, with a taste of the islands.

1 cup yogurt
1 tablespoon lemon juice
1/2 cup pineapple juice
1/4 cup canned, crushed pineapple
1 tablespoon honey
2 egg whites

Combine all except egg whites.
Beat egg whites in separate bowl until stiff peaks form.
Fold whites into yogurt mixture.
Cover and freeze until slushy.
Sprinkle with flaked coconut and chopped macadamia nuts. (Both
optional).

§ Fruit With Yogurt-Ginger Sauce §
(Serves 1)

Tropical fruits and creamy-smooth yogurt, with a tart touch of ginger, create a delicious, light dessert.

1/4 cup pineapple chunks
2 tablespoons flaked coconut
1/2 banana, chopped
1 teaspoon chopped fresh ginger
2 tablespoons plain, low-fat yogurt (or sour cream, if preferred)
1 teaspoon honey
1 teaspoon orange or pineapple juice

Mix all ingredients, chill and serve.

§ Low Cholesterol Banana-Pineapple Cookies §

Even when you are avoiding foods with cholesterol, you can have a touch of sweetness with these cake-like puffs.

1 egg white
1/4 cup mashed ripe banana (1/2 medium banana)
1/4 cup crushed pineapple with juice
1/4 cup polyunsaturated vegetable oil
1 tablespoon skim milk
1 cup flour
1 tablespoon brown sugar
1/4 teaspoon baking soda
1/4 teaspoon salt
1/4 teaspoon cloves
1/4 cup flaked coconut

Preheat oven to 350°.
Mix egg white, banana, pineapple, oil and milk.
Beat in all other ingredients.
Place by spoonfuls on baking sheet.
Bake 8-10 minutes, until golden brown. (Do not overcook; the
cookies should be light in color.)

Supermarket Service

Most supermarkets and grocery stores will help with extra service, if you request it. If you want just half a squash or cabbage; if you prefer only 1 lamb chop or 1/2 pound of ground
beef; if you'd like 6 eggs instead of a dozen—ask. The clerk
or butcher is there to serve you.

Section Two

MENUS

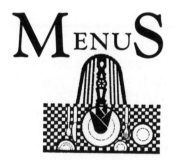

In these day-by-day menus, dishes with recipes in Section 1 are marked in bold print, and the page number of the recipe is indicated in parentheses.

You may wish to follow the menus in the order given, or pick and choose from the recipes you prefer.

Coffee, tea, and milk have not been included in the menus, but they may be added to each meal. It's a good idea to serve water with every meal, as well!.

WEEK 1

Sunday Breakfast

Light Menu

Orange Juice with squeeze of Lemon
Whole Wheat Toast with Peanut Butter and sprinkle of Cinnamon

Hearty Menu

Orange Juice with squeeze of Lemon
Eggs Benedict (page85)

Sunday Dinner

Light Menu

Tomato Juice with Dash of Hot Pepper Sauce
Tasty Tuna (page 71)
Minty Fruit Salad (page 127)
Bernice's Oatmeal Cookies (page 141)

Hearty Menu

One-Pot Pot Roast (page 15)
Minty Fruit Salad (page 127)
Bernice's Oatmeal Cookies (page 141)

Monday Breakfast

Light Menu

1/2 Grapefruit, cut into chunks
Instant Hot Cereal with Milk and Honey or Brown Sugar

Hearty Menu

1/2 Grapefruit, cut into chunks
French Toast with Butter or Margarine and Syrup or Fruit
  Pureé

Monday Dinner

Light Menu

Easy Quiche (page 86)
Tossed Green Salad with Favorite Dressing
Applesauce

Hearty Menu

Meat and Potatoes (page 16)
Pineapple-Carrots (page 116)
Tossed Green Salad with Favorite Dressing
Applesauce and Cookies

Tuesday Breakfast

Light Menu

Tangerine Segments
Bran Muffin with Butter, Margarine, or Cream Cheese and Jam

Hearty Menu

Pineapple Juice with scoop of Pineapple Sherbet
Cornmeal Biscuits (page 97) with Butter or Margarine
Sausage Links

Tuesday Dinner

Light Menu

Mushroom-Zucchini Frittata (page 84)
Steamed Green Beans with Dill and Grated Cheese
French Bread with Butter or Margarine

Hearty Menu

Baked Chicken (page 44)
Baked Potato, topped with Yogurt and Chives
Green Beans Parmesan (page 117)
Flavored Gelatin with Fruit

Wednesday Breakfast

Light Menu

Plain, Low-Fat Yogurt with Chopped Fruit, sprinkled with Granola
(or other fiber-rich cereal)
Orange-Honey Loaf (page 101)

Hearty Menu

Pineapple Juice
Scrambled Eggs with Grated Cheese and Chives
Orange-Honey Loaf (page 101)

Wednesday Dinner

Light Menu

Penny's Thousand-Year Chicken Soup (page 54)
French Bread, toasted
Tomato Slices with Chopped Parsely

Hearty Menu

Cranberry Pork Steaks (page 34)
Buttered Corn (canned, frozen or fresh)
Tomato and Cucumber Slices with Chopped Parsley
French Bread, toasted
Betty's Lemon Cake Pudding (page 133)

Thursday Breakfast

Light Menu

Cottage Cheese with Crushed Pineapple and Dash of Ginger
Super-Muffins (page 95)

Hearty Menu

Grapefruit Juice
Hot Cereal with Raisins, Milk, and Honey
Super-Muffins (page 95)

Thursday Dinner

Light Menu

Cheese Soubise (page 84)
Grated Carrot Salad (page 127)
Tangerine

Hearty Menu

Pineapple Sweet-and-Sour Pork (page 35)
Grated Carrot Salad (page 127)
White or Brown Rice
Tangerine

Friday Breakfast

Light Menu

Melon Wedge with Squeeze of Lemon
Oatmeal Cookie Spread with Peanut Butter

Hearty Menu

Melon Wedge with squeeze of Lemon
Frozen, Toasted Waffles with Butter or Margarine and Syrup or
    Fruit Pureé
Baked Ham Slice, heated

Friday Dinner

Light Menu

Garden Stew (page 117)
Cornmeal Biscuits (page 97)
Prune-Apple Bars (page 144)

Hearty Menu

Fish with Herbs (page 62)
Rice, white or brown, with chopped Almonds and Parsley
Chopped Lettuce Salad with Tomato Wedges
Prune-Apple Bars (page 144)

Saturday Breakfast

Light Menu

Cereal Parfait (Cold Cereal, Chopped Fruit, and Ice Cream layered in a parfait glass)

Hearty Menu

Orange Juice
Egg-in-a-Nest (page 87)

Saturday Dinner

Light Menu

Creamy Tomato Soup (page 115)
Oyster Crackers
Mixed Green Salad: Lettuce, Spinach, and Green Pepper with Lemon Juice

Hearty Menu

Prime-Time Pizza (page 28)
Finger-Food Salad (Carrot and Celery Sticks with Chunks of Broccoli and Green Bell Pepper)
Peanut Butter Squares (page 144)

WEEK 2

Sunday Breakfast

Light Menu

Prune Juice
Poached Egg on Rye Toast

Hearty Menu

Stewed Prunes
Hot Cereal with Chopped Apples, Raisins, and Cinnamon

Sunday Dinner

Light Menu

Ginger-Coconut Chicken (page 45)
Mixed Salad with Dressing: Lettuce, Cucumber, Parsley, and
    Tomato
Lemon Sherbet (page 142)

Hearty Menu

Jambalaya Chicken (page 52)
Dinner Roll with Butter or Margarine
Chopped Lettuce Salad with Dressing
Lemon or Orange Sherbet (page 142)

Monday Breakfast

Light Menu

Orange Slice with Flaked Coconut
Cold Cereal and Milk topped with Sliced Banana and dash of
  Allspice

Hearty Menu

Orange Slice with Flaked Coconut
Onion-Pepper Omelet (page 80)
Whole Wheat Toast with Butter or Margarine and Jam

Monday Dinner

Light Menu

Chicken-Stuffed Tomato (page 53)
Biscuit or Whole Wheat Toast with Butter or Margarine

Hearty Menu

Chicken Cobbler (page 53)
Coleslaw with Pineapple and Carrots (page 125)
Apple-Cran Crisp (page 136)

Tuesday Breakfast

Light Menu

Peachy Banana Shake (page 129)

Hearty Menu

Peachy Banana Shake (page 129)
Whole Wheat Toast with Butter or Margarine
Slice of Cooked Ham, heated

Tuesday Dinner

Light Menu

Fish Fillet Vinaigrette (page 61)
Sliced Tomatoes with Dill
French Bread with Garlic Butter

Hearty Menu

Spicy Fish Stew (page 67)
Tossed Green Salad with Dressing and Dill
Pineapple Betty (page 134)

Wednesday Breakfast

Light Menu

Cranberry Juice
Whole Wheat Toast with Butter or Margarine
Slice of Cooked Ham

Hearty Menu

Cranberry Juice
Eggs with Corn and Bacon (page 88)
Whole Wheat Toast with Butter or Margarine

Wednesday Dinner

Light Menu

Tuna On a Muffin (page 73)
Carrot and Celery Sticks
1/2 **Frozen Banana** (page 129)

Hearty Menu

Pineapple Pork Chops (page 34)
Brown Rice
Steamed Broccoli
1/2 **Frozen Banana** (page 129)

Thursday Breakfast

Light Menu

Pineapple Danish (page 99)

Hearty Menu

Orange Juice
Spicy Baked Pancake (page 105)

Thursday Dinner

Light Menu

Supper Salad (page 38)
French Bread, toasted, with Butter or Margarine
Cherry Crumb Crunch (page 147)

Hearty Menu

Tuna-Vegie Dish (page 72)
Carrot-Raisin Salad (page 122)
French Bread, toasted, with Butter or Margarine
Cherry Crumb Crunch (page 147)

Friday Breakfast

Light Menu

1/2 Grapefruit drizzled with Honey
Toasted English Muffin with Peanut Butter

Hearty Menu

1/2 Grapefruit drizzled with Honey
Toasted English Muffin
Poached Egg
2 Slices Bacon, fried to taste

Friday Dinner

Light Menu

Shrimp-Corn Curry (page 74)
Best-Yet Walnut Bread (page 103)

Hearty Menu

Stuffed Green Peppers (page 26)
Spinach Salad with Oil and Vinegar Dressing
Best-Yet Walnut Bread (page 103)

Saturday Breakfast

Light Menu

Pineapple Eggnog (page 79)
Whole Wheat Toast with Butter or Margarine

Hearty Menu

Blueberry Flummery (page 134)
Hazel's Quick Coffee Cake (page 98)
Scrambled Eggs with Cheese and Dill

Saturday Dinner

Light Menu

Turkey Parmesan (page 55)
Cranberry Sauce
Steamed Green Peas sprinkled with Chopped Mint
Star Cookies (page 146)

Hearty Menu

Stuffed Cornish Game Hen (page 48)
Brown Rice with dash of **Mixed Herbs** (page 9)
Steamed Green Peas sprinkled with Chopped Mint
Caramel Custard (page 135)

WEEK 3

Sunday Breakfast

Light Menu

Prune Whip (page 140)

Hearty Menu

Prune Juice
Hot Cereal with Raisins and Chopped Dates

Sunday Dinner

Light Menu

Succotash Ham (page 37)
Tossed Green Salad with French Dressing
Peanut Butter Squares (page 144)

Hearty Menu

Ham-Stuffed Squash (page 38)
Tossed Green Salad with Cucumber and Tomato Slices
Chocolate Applesauce Cake (page 148)

Monday Breakfast

Light Menu

Orange Juice
Bagel with Cream Cheese and Jam

Hearty Menu

Orange Juice
Whole Wheat Toast with Butter or Margarine
Onion-Pepper Omelet (page 80)

Monday Dinner

Light Menu

Turkey Patties (page 56)
Tomato Wedges on Lettuce, sprinkled with Lemon Juice
Hot French Bread
Fresh Orange Segments

Hearty Menu

Oriental Beef (page 21)
Rice
Steamed Broccoli
Fresh Orange Segments

Tuesday Breakfast

Light Menu

Tomato Juice with Dash of Hot Pepper Sauce
Super-Muffins (page 95)

Hearty Menu

Prune Whip (page 140)
Super-Muffins with Peanut Butter (page 95)

Tuesday Dinner

Light Menu

Tomato-Egg Bake (page 82)
Slice of Rye Bread with Butter or Margarine
Blueberry Sweet Bread (page 102)

Hearty Menu

Fish in Mushroom Cream Sauce (page 63)
Grated Carrot Salad (page 127)
Blueberry Sweet Bread (page 102)

Wednesday Breakfast

Light Menu

Applesauce with Raisins
Whole Wheat Toast with Butter or Margarine

Hearty Menu

Baked Apple (page 128)
Wheat Sticks (page 97)

Wednesday Dinner

Light Menu

French Onion Soup (page 114)
Mixed Fresh Greens—Lettuce, Spinach, Kale, Parsley
Macaroon Torte (page 137)

Hearty Menu

Chicken Liver Special (page 46)
Waldorf Delight (page 123)
Hot French Bread
Steamed Carrots
Macaroon Torte (page 137)

Thursday Breakfast

Light Menu

Yogurt with Chopped Fresh Fruit or Berries

Hearty Menu

Fruit or Berries with Milk
Broccoli and Egg (page 82)

Thursday Dinner

Light Menu

Onions au Gratin (page 111)
Apple-Carrot Slaw (page 123)

Hearty Menu

Turkey Tetrazzini (page 55)
Apple-Carrot Slaw (page 123)
Lemon or Orange Sherbet (page 142)

Friday Breakfast

Light Menu

Grapefruit Juice
Whole Wheat Toast with Cheese Slice

Hearty Menu

Grapefruit Juice
Cranberry Pears (page 128)
Toast with Grated or Sliced Cheese

Friday Dinner

Light Menu

Double Cheese Pudding (page 87)
Chopped Lettuce Salad with French Dressing
Rye Crackers
Fresh Pear, quartered

Hearty Menu

Macaroni and Cheese (page 80) with Ham Cubes
Chopped Lettuce Salad with French Dressing
Fresh Pear, quartered
Oat Wheat Cookies (page 140)

Saturday Breakfast

Light Menu

Pineapple Juice
Pineapple Danish (page 99)

Hearty Menu

Fruit Compote (mixture of fresh and canned fruits)
Whole Wheat Toast with Butter or Margarine
Slice of Hot, Cooked Ham

Saturday Dinner

Light Menu

Mildred's Tomato-Cheese Soup (page 110)
Crackers
1/2 sliced Banana

Hearty Menu

Dilly Yogurt Fish (page 64)
Pineapple Beets (page 112)
Carrot Sticks
Apple Spice Cake (page 136)

WEEK 4

Sunday Breakfast

Light Menu

Orange Wheel Slices with Flaked Coconut
Whole Wheat Toast with Peanut Butter and Honey

Hearty Menu

Orange Slices with flaked Coconut
Eggs Benedict (page 85)

Sunday Dinner

Light Menu

Chicken a' la King (page 44)
Granny's Baking Powder Biscuits (page 104)
Steamed Peas, fresh or frozen
Hawaiian Ice (page 152)

Hearty Menu

Chicken Curry (page 41)
Rice
Tossed Green Salad with Dressing
Hawaiian Ice (page 152)

Monday Breakfast

Light Menu

Cold Cereal with Milk and Chopped Banana

Hearty Menu

Hot Cereal with Milk, Honey, Raisins, and Chopped Fresh or
  Frozen Fruit

Monday Dinner

Light Menu

Supper Salad (page 38)
Hot French Bread

Hearty Menu

"No-Peek" Stew (page 17)
Granny's Baking Powder Biscuits (page 104)
Sliced Tomatoes with Salad Dressing
Fresh or Canned Fruit

Tuesday Breakfast

Light Menu

Pineapple Eggnog (page 79)

Hearty Menu

Prune Juice
Whole Wheat Toast with Butter or Margarine
Scrambled Eggs with Ham Bits and Chives or Green Onions

Tuesday Dinner

Light Menu

Spicy Fish Stew (page 67)
Whole Wheat Toast
Chocolate Pudding (see **Pudding Mix** page 139)

Hearty Menu

Vegetable-Rice (page 112)
Fruit Salad: Orange, Banana, and Apple Sections on Lettuce
Chocolate Pudding (see **Pudding Mix** page 139)

Wednesday Breakfast

Light Menu

Yogurt with Chopped Banana and Frozen Blueberries

Hearty Menu

Cinnamon Apple Pudding hot, with milk (page 149)

Wednesday Dinner

Light Menu

Mushroom-Zucchini Frittata (page 84)
Cornmeal Biscuits (page 97)
Cookie

Hearty Menu

Meat Loaf (page 21)
Coleslaw with Pineapple and Carrots (page 125)
Aunt Esther's Wacky Cake (page 138)

Thursday Breakfast

Light Menu

Orange Juice
Super-Muffins (page 95)

Hearty Menu

Orange Juice
Bacon and Potato Eggs (page 90)
Whole Wheat Toast with Butter or Margarine and Jam

Thursday Dinner

Light Menu

Lentil Soup (page 122)
Crackers
Tossed Green Salad with Dressing
Fresh or Canned Pears

Hearty Menu

Lo-Cal Turkey Breast (page 57)
Chilled Bean Salad (page 124)
Fresh or Canned Pears

Friday Breakfast

Light Menu

Peachy Banana Shake (page 129)

Hearty Menu

Peaches with Flaked Coconut
Cheese Puffs (page 91)

Friday Dinner

Light Menu

Tuna au Gratin (page 74)
Minty Fruit Salad (page 127)

Hearty Menu

Ginger Snapper (page 65)
Minty Fruit Salad (page 127)
White or Brown Rice
Steamed Green Beans
Star Cookies (page 146)

Saturday Breakfast

Light Menu

Grape Yogurt Fluff (page 150)

Hearty Menu

Grape Yogurt Fluff (page 150)
Hot Oat Cereal with Milk and Brown Sugar

Saturday Dinner

Light Menu

Fried Rice (page 118)
Carrot-Raisin Salad (page 122)

Hearty Menu

Chicken Milano (page 49)
Carrot-Raisin Salad (page 122)
Vera's Fresh Strawberry Pie (page 146)

WEEK 5

Sunday Breakfast

Light Menu

Grape Juice
Edith's Oatmeal Cookies (page 148) with Peanut Butter

Hearty Menu

Applesauce
Frozen, Toasted Waffle with jam or pureed fruit
2 Strips Bacon

Sunday Dinner

Light Menu

Beef 'n Beans (page 22)
Rye Bread with Butter or Margarine
Spinach Salad with Chopped, Hardcooked Eggs
Yogurt Banana Split (page 152)

Hearty Menu

"Yoganoff" with Zucchini (page 16)
Noodles
Spinach Salad
Yogurt Banana Split (page 152)
Star Cookie (page 146)

Monday Breakfast

Light Menu

Orange Juice
Blueberry Oatmeal Muffins (page 104)

Hearty Menu

Orange Juice
Scrambled Egg with Dill and Chopped Green Onion
Blueberry Oatmeal Muffins (page 104)

Monday Dinner

Light Menu

Sausage Pepper Saute' (page 36)
Sliced Tomato
Apple-Cran Crisp (page 136)

Hearty Menu

Midwest Pork Chops (page 33)
Sliced Tomato on Lettuce with Sweet Basil
Mashed Potatoes
Apple-Cran Crisp (page 136)

Tuesday Breakfast

Light Menu

Prune Juice
Egg-in-a-Nest (page 87)

Hearty Menu

Stewed Prunes with Apple Chunks
Oatcakes (page 100) with Maple Syrup or Jam

Tuesday Dinner

Light Menu

Stir-Fried Chicken (page 47)
White or Brown Rice
Tangerine, peeled and sectioned

Hearty Menu

Salad Dressing Chicken (page 50)
Carrot and Celery Sticks
Baked Potato with Butter or Margarine or Yogurt
Tangerine segments

Wednesday Breakfast

Light Menu

1/2 Grapefruit sprinkled with sugar
Super-Muffins (page 95)

Hearty Menu

1/2 Grapefruit sprinkled with sugar
Scramble Eggs with Bacon
Whole Wheat Toast with Marmalade

Wednesday Dinner

Light Menu

Chicken Salad (page 43)
Hot **Cornmeal Biscuit** (page 97)
Applesauce sprinkled with Ginger Snap Crumbs

Hearty Menu

Chicken Cobbler (page 53)
Tossed Green Salad with Ranch-Style dressing
Frozen Fruity Yogurt (page 151)

Thursday Breakfast

Light Menu

Pineapple Juice
Whole Wheat Toast with Cinnamon, Brown Sugar, and
  Chopped Nuts.

Hearty Menu

Pineapple Juice
Hot Cereal with Oat Bran, Cinnamon, Raisins, and Brown Sugar

Thursday Dinner

Light Menu

Tuna Chowder (page 71)
Rye Toast, with or without Caraway
Green Pepper and Carrot Salad with Oil and Vinegar Dressing

Hearty Menu

Swiss Steak Special (page 20)
Mashed or Roasted Potatoes
Green Pepper and Carrot Salad

Friday Breakfast

Light Menu

Frozen Fruity Yogurt (page 151) sprinkled with Crushed Dry
Cereal (corn or wheat flakes)

Hearty Menu

Grapefruit Juice
Orange-Honey Loaf slice (page 101)
Scrambled Eggs with Grated Cheese

Friday Dinner

Light Menu

Egg Foo Yung (page 90)
White or Brown Rice
Sliced Orange

Hearty Menu

Chili Hash (page 23)
Cornmeal Biscuits (page 97)
Sliced cucumbers with Dill
Edith's Oatmeal Cookies (page 148)
Sliced Orange

Saturday Breakfast

Light Menu

Orange Juice
Poached Egg on Whole Wheat Toast

Hearty Menu

Orange Juice
Soft-boiled Egg
Whole Wheat Toast with Butter or Margarine and Jam
Sausage Patties

Saturday Dinner

Light Menu

Mashed Potatoes Plus (page 109)
Steamed Broccoli
Mixed Fruit Compote

Hearty Menu

Lentils and Rice (page 121)
Steamed Broccoli topped with Grated Cheese
Mixed Fruit Compote and Cookies

WEEK 6

Sunday Breakfast

Light Menu

Pineapple Eggnog (page 79)

Hearty Menu

Pineapple Juice
Baked Potato Topped with Bacon Bits and Grated Cheese

Sunday Dinner

Light Menu

Foil Fish (page 67)
Ginger Carrots (page 110)
Chopped Spinach Salad

Hearty Menu

Baked Fish with Mushrooms and Tomato (page 66)
Boiled Potatoes
Chopped Spinach Salad
Apple Spice Cake (page 136)

Monday Breakfast

Light Menu

Cold Cereal with Milk and Chopped Berries, Peaches or Banana

Hearty Menu

Yogurt Banana Split (page 152)
Toasted English Muffin with Butter or Margarine

Monday Dinner

Light Menu

Corn Pudding (page 83)
Steamed Peas, garnished with Chopped Mint Leaves
Peanut Butter Squares (page 144)

Hearty Menu

Spanish Rice (page 120)
Tossed Green Salad with Cucumber Slices
Peanut Butter Square (page 144)

Tuesday Breakfast

Light Menu

Applesauce Topped with Chopped Nuts and Raisins
Whole Wheat Toast with Butter or Margarine

Hearty Menu

Grapefruit Juice
Frozen Toasted Waffles with Jam, Fruit Pureé or Applesauce
Lean Cooked Ham Slice

Tuesday Dinner

Light Menu

Swiss Eggs (page 81)
Tomato, Cucumber, and Radish Salad

Hearty Menu

Hamburger Stew (page 28)
Tomato, Cucumber, and Radish Salad
Granny's Baking Powder Biscuits (page 104)
Hawaiian Ice (page 152)

Wednesday Breakfast

Light Menu

Prune Juice
Yogurt with Chopped Dates, Raisins, topped with Crushed Cereal
　(Granola or corn or wheat flakes)

Hearty Menu

Stewed Prunes with Lemon Wedge
Cheese Omelet
Whole Wheat Toast with Butter or Margarine

Wednesday Dinner

Light Menu

Potato-Onion Soup (page 116)
Apple-Carrot Slaw (page 123)
Rye Crackers

Hearty Menu

Chicken Cacciatore (page 42)
Noodles
Steamed Green Beans with Rosemary
Cherry Crumb Crunch (page 147)

Thursday Breakfast

Light Menu

Peachy Banana Shake (page 129)

Hearty Menu

Fresh or Canned Peaches
French Toast with Butter and Syrup or Brown Sugar

Thursday Dinner

Light Menu

Spicy Red Snapper (page 65)
French Bread
Peach Half with Scoop of Cottage Cheese, on Lettuce
Best-Yet Walnut Bread (page 103)

Hearty Menu

Fish On Spinach (page 68)
Ginger Carrots (page 110)
Baked Potato
Best-Yet Walnut Bread (page 103)

Friday Breakfast

Light Menu

Orange Juice
Bed-and-Breakfast Bran Muffins (page 96)

Hearty Menu

Orange Juice
Bed-and-Breakfast Bran Muffins (page 96)
Chopped Ham, Stir-Fried and mixed with Pineapple chunks

Friday Dinner

Light Menu

Chicken-Stuffed Tomato (page 53)
Hot French Bread
Prune-Apple Bars (page 144)

Hearty Menu

Chicken Parmesan (page 51)
Baked Potato
Steamed Celery chunks with Sweet Basil
Prune-Apple Bars (page 144)

Saturday Breakfast

Light Menu

Prune Whip (page 140)

Hearty Menu

Prune Whip (page 140)
Oatcakes (page 100) with Butter or Margarine and Syrup

Saturday Dinner

Light Menu

Chili Cheese (page 89)
Sliced Green Pepper and Red Onion with Oil and Vinegar
  Salad Dressing
Frozen Banana Chunks (page 129)

Hearty Menu

Carolyn's Ratatouille (page 119)
Hot French Bread with Garlic Butter
Cinnamon Apple Pudding (page 149) with **Dessert
Topping** (page 137)

APPENDIX I:

Low-to-Moderate Sodium Recipes

Health experts say that most of us take in more sodium than we need: from 2,300 to 6,900 milligrams per day. An adequate sodium intake per day for an adult is far less: 1,100 to 3,300 milligrams, according to the National Research Council.

Most of the sodium in our diet comes from sodium chloride, better known as table salt. One teaspoon of salt contains about 2,000 milligrams of salt. Salt is second only to sugar as a food additive. Sodium is also found in other common ingredients and additives such as baking soda, baking powder, sodium nitrite, and monosodium glutamate (MSG).

Too much sodium may contribute to high blood pressure, so many scientists and physicians recommend that we eat less of it. The best way is to cut down on salt. A few hints on decreasing sodium:
—Avoid "convenience foods", unless labeled low-sodium. Most frozen and canned dishes, such as pizzas, TV dinners, pies, and soups, have high amounts of sodium.
—Read labels on packaged foods and learn to recognize ingredients that contain sodium: salt, soy sauce, and soda, for example.
—Reduce or cut out the amount of salt in cooking.

—At the table, taste food before you add salt—or take the shaker off the table and use other flavor-enhancers instead, such as lemon juice, vinegar, and herbs.

Many of the recipes in this book are low to moderate in sodium content. Those that are especially low in sodium are listed on the following page. Many others may be adjusted to lower-sodium diets simply by omitting salt and avoiding canned ingredients, which almost always contain sodium.

Herbs are creative, flavorful alternatives to salt. They can turn simple foods into gourmet delights that tempt the appetite and please the palate. Replace the salt in your diet with other seasonings and help keep your blood pressure down while you enhance your dining pleasure.

The following chart will help you choose which herbs and spices to use:

Beef	Bay leaf, chives, cloves, cumin, garlic, marjoram, rosemary, savory, thyme, pepper, nutmeg.
Chicken	Lemon, garlic, sage, thyme, paprika, marjoram, rosemary, oregano, savory.
Fish	Lemon, curry powder, dry mustard, marjoram, chervil, dill, fennel, tarragon, garlic, parsley, thyme.
Lamb	Rosemary, garlic, ginger, pepper, savory, thyme, coriander, sage, mint, curry powder.
Pork	Cumin, garlic, ginger, pepper, savory, thyme, coriander, sage.
Cheese	Sweet basil, chervil, chives, curry, garlic, marjoram, dill, parsley, oregano, thyme.
Eggs	Sweet basil, dill, parsley, savory.
Bread	Caraway, poppy seed, marjoram, thyme.
Asparagus	Lemon, garlic.
Beans	Dill, lemon, marjoram, nutmeg.
Cucumbers	Chives, dill, garlic, vinegar.
Peas	Mint, parsley.
Potatoes	Chives, paprika, parsley, mace.
Squash	Cinnamon, ginger, mace, nutmeg.
Tomatoes	Sweet basil, marjoram, oregano, dill.
Fruits	Cinnamon, cloves, ginger, mint.

Recipes in this book which are low or moderate in sodium are:

APPENDIX II:

Low-Cholesterol Recipes

The latest evidence in nutritional studies show that we have a better chance of preventing cardiovascular disease if we eat foods that are low in cholesterol or help reduce it. Cholesterol is a fatty substance that can clog arteries, preventing the blood from flowing freely.

Many of the dishes in this book are low in cholesterol; the lowest are listed below. You can lower cholesterol intake even further by substituting low-cholesterol ingredients for high ones. The following charts show the foods to choose or avoid.

Check with your doctor if you are concerned about the cholesterol level in your diet.

Foods High in Cholesterol

Butter, lard, hard margarine
Coconut, peanut and palm oils (read labels for ingredients;
    many prepared foods contain these oils)
Salt pork, bacon, red meats
Gravies and sauces made with cream and/or cheese
All milk except skim
Whole-milk cheese
Egg yolk
Frankfurters, sausage, lunch meats
Poultry skin
Organ meats: heart, liver, brains,
    kidney
Corned beef, spareribs

Frozen packaged dinners
Commercial biscuit and cake mixes, except angel food cake
Potato and corn chips, flavored crackers, pretzels
Sweet rolls, doughnuts, commercial cake and bread mixes
Cream soups
Avocado

Pies, cakes, cookies containing whole milk or egg yolk
Ice cream, ice milk, whipped cream, most non-dairy creamers
Chocolate, coconut, most candies
Cashew and macadamia nuts
Condiments: catsup, soy sauce, steak sauce, pickles, mustard

Foods Low in Cholesterol

Margarine high in polyunsaturated fats, such as:
    Fleishmann's
    Mazola
    Nucoa
    Saffola
    Chiffon (soft tub)
Safflower, corn, cotton seed, and soybean oils
Non-dairy coffee creamers that contain soybean oil
Oats and oat bran
Lean meats and poultry
Fresh or frozen vegetables
Fresh or frozen fruits
Fish and shellfish
Wheat bran and corn bran
Garlic
Dried beans and peas
Egg whites
Dry curd cottage cheese, low-fat cheese
Skim milk, low-fat yogurt, skimmed buttermilk
Barley, rice, pasta
Gelatin, sherbet, pudding made with skim milk, angel food cake
Homemade soups
Vinegar, herbs, spices, honey, jam, syrup

Recipes in this book which are low in cholesterol are:

DO YOU HAVE A FRIEND OR RELATIVE
WHO WOULD ENJOY THIS BOOK?

Use the convenient order form below.

YES,
    please send __ copies of THE OLDER AMERICANS COOKBOOK.

        _____   Hardcover: $16.95 each.

        _____   Paperback: $8.95 each.

        _____   Comb-bound (lies flat): $10.95 each.

Add $1.50 postage for the first book; $.50 for each additional book.

NAME: _____

ADDRESS: _____

_____

                                   ZIP:

Please fill in the above information and send with your check or money order (do not send cash) to:

Tudor Publishers, Inc.
P.O. Box 3443
Greensboro, North Carolina 27402

Allow 4-6 weeks for delivery. Prices subject to change without notice.

Our Guarantee: You must be completely satisfied or return the book in undamaged condition within 30 days for a full refund.